First Workshop on Eye-tracking and Natural Language Processing

Held at the 24th International Conference on Computational Linguistics (COLING 2012)

Mumbai, India
15 December 2012

Editors:

Michael Carl
Pushpak Bhattacharya
Kamal Kumar Choudhary

ISBN: 978-1-62748-350-6

Printed from e-media with permission by:

Curran Associates, Inc.
57 Morehouse Lane
Red Hook, NY 12571

Some format issues inherent in the e-media version may also appear in this print version.

Printed by Curran Associates, Inc. (2013)

Association for Computational Linguistics
209 N. Eighth Street
Stroudsburg, Pennsylvania 18360

Phone: 1-570-476-8006
Fax: 1-570-476-0860

acl@aclweb.org

Additional copies of this publication are available from:

Curran Associates, Inc.
57 Morehouse Lane
Red Hook, NY 12571 USA
Phone: 845-758-0400
Fax: 845-758-2634
Email: curran@proceedings.com
Web: www.proceedings.com

COLING 2012

24th International Conference on Computational Linguistics

Proceedings of the First Workshop on Eye-tracking and Natural Language Processing

Workshop chairs:
Michael Carl, Pushpak Bhattacharya and
Kamal Kumar Choudhary

15 December 2012
Mumbai, India

Preface

The workshop "Eye-tracking and Natural Language Processing" (ETNLP) is an exploratory ½ satelite workshop in the context of Coling 2012, Mumbai. Over the last decades, eye-tracking system have been used for reading research, human-computer interaction, user modeling and usability studies, system evaluation and feature extraction, as well as for on-line applications such as real-time human-machine interaction, intelligent user adaptation and gaze-based control.

The ETNLP workshop sets out to explore the state of the art in eye-tracking techniques and Natural Language Processing. Given the interdisciplinary nature of the workshop, we invited papers on all topics related to gaze-based language and/or reading research, gaze-based computational psycholinguistics, eye movements and attention in natural language understanding, corpora of gaze data in language processing and other, so as to foster and explore eye-tracking methods in modeling natural language processing.

We received eight submissions relevant to the theme of the workshop from different part of the world. All submissions were reviewed in a double-blind process by three reviewers and finally five papers were accepted for presentation. In addition to the five papers, we invited Matthew Crocker, Saarland University, to talk about his eye-tracking research on spoken interaction. These presentations cover a broad area of topics, including processing effort in reading, parsing and translation, models on linguistic complexity and surprisal, investigation into classification of scanpaths and systematic error correction, as well as gaze behavior in dialog and spoken interaction. A plethora of experimental and computational methods are used and introduced to analyze the gaze data, such as a morpho-syntactic surprisal index, a scasim measure, the dirac delta and conditional random fields. Many of the contributions show a tendency to enlarge the scope of the processing units, moving from single word fixations to scan paths, syntactic chunks, the reading line, usage of micro and macro units, etc. so as to capture more general gaze-movement and text processing strategies.

The workshop provides an opportunity for researcher to present their work and to interact with peers around the world in this emerging field of research. It is an opportunity for people working in different field such as Computational Linguistics, Psycholinguistics, and Computational Psycholinguistics to come together and share their views on Eye-tracking and Natural Language Processing.

The workshop organizers would like to thank the authors for their contributions and the programme committee for their review work. Special thanks goes to the Coling organizers, who made this event possible.

We look forward to seeing you all at ETNLP 2012

Michael Carl, Pushpak Bhattacharyya, Kamal Kumar Choudhary

ETNLP 2012 Workshop Organizers

Organizers:

Michael Carl (Copenhagen Business School, Denmark)
Pushpak Bhattacharya (IIT Mumbai, India)
Kamal Kumar Choudhary (IIT Ropar, India)

Invited Speaker:

Matthew Crocker (Saarland University, Germany)

Programme Committee:

Pushpak Bhattacharyya (IIT Mumbai, India)
Ralf Biedert (DFKI, Germany)
Sharon O'Brien (DCU, Ireland)
Michael Carl (Copenhagen Business School, Denmark)
Kamal Kumar Choudhary (IIT Ropar, India)
Matthew Crocker (Saarland University, Germany)
Silvia Hansen-Schirra (University of Mainz, Germany)
Kenneth Holmqvist (Humanities Lab, Sweden)
Sam Hutton (SR-research, Canada)
Frank Keller (University of Edinburgh)
Pascual Martinez (University of Tokyo, Japan)
Ricardo Matos (Tobii, Sweden)
Mattias Nilsson (Uppsala University, Sweden)
Kari-Jouko Räihä (University of Tampere, Finland)
RMK Sinha (JSS Academy of Technical Education, India)
Oleg Spakov (University of Tampere, Finland)
Sara Stymne (Linköping University, Sweden)
Per Henning Uppstad (Lesecenteret, Norway)

Table of Contents

Grounding spoken interaction with real-time gaze in dynamic virtual environments
Matthew Crocker 1

Identifying instances of processing effort in translation through heat maps: an eye-tracking study using multiple input sources
Fabio Alves, José Luiz Gonçalves and Karina Szpak 5

Robustness and processing difficulty models. A pilot study for eye-tracking data on the French Treebank
Stéphane Rauzy and Philippe Blache 21

Scanpaths in reading are informative about sentence processing
Titus von der Malsburg, Shravan Vasishth and Reinhold Kliegl 37

Predicting Word Fixations in Text with a CRF Model for Capturing General Reading Strategies among Readers
Tadayoshi Hara, Daichi Mochihashi, Yoshinobu Kano and Akiko Aizawa 55

A heuristic-based approach for systematic error correction of gaze data for reading
Abhijit Mishra, Michael Carl and Pushpak Bhattacharyya 71

First Workshop on Eye-tracking and Natural Language Processing

Program

Saturday, 15 December 2012

09:30–10:20	**Invited talk:** *Grounding spoken interaction with real-time gaze in dynamic virtual environments* Matthew Crocker
10:20–10:45	*Identifying instances of processing effort in translation through heat maps: an eye-tracking study using multiple input sources* Fabio Alves, José Luiz Gonçalves and Karina Szpak
10:45–11:10	*Robustness and processing difficulty models. A pilot study for eye-tracking data on the French Treebank* Stéphane Rauzy and Philippe Blache
11:10–12:00	Tea break
12:00–12:25	*Scanpaths in reading are informative about sentence processing* Titus von der Malsburg, Shravan Vasishth and Reinhold Kliegl
12:25–12:50	*Predicting Word Fixations in Text with a CRF Model for Capturing General Reading Strategies among Readers* Tadayoshi Hara, Daichi Mochihashi, Yoshinobu Kano and Akiko Aizawa
12:50–13:15	*A heuristic-based approach for systematic error correction of gaze data for reading* Abhijit Mishra, Michael Carl and Pushpak Bhattacharyya

Grounding spoken interaction with real-time gaze in dynamic virtual environments

Matthew Crocker
Saarland University
`crocker@coli.uni-saarland.de`

ABSTRACT

Gaze is an important cue in visually situated dialog, grounding referring expressions to objects in the environment. We present a new technique which demonstrates that monitoring real-time listener gaze – and giving appropriate feedback – enhances reference resolution by the listener: In a 3D virtual environment, users followed directional instructions, including pressing a number of buttons that were identified using referring expression generated by the system (see GIVE; Koller et al., 2010). Gaze to the intended referent following a referring expression was taken as evidence of successful understanding and elicited positive feedback; by contrast, gaze to other objects triggered early negative feedback.

We compared this eye movement-based feedback strategy with two baseline systems, revealing that the eye-movement based feedback leads to significantly more successful button presses than the other two strategies. Our findings suggest that listener gaze immediately following a referring expression reliably indicates how a listener resolved the expression.

KEYWORDS : visually situated dialog, spoken interaction, referring expressions, eye-tracking

Introduction

The interactive nature of dialogue entails that interlocutors are constantly anticipating what will be said next and speakers are monitoring the effects of their utterances on listeners. Gaze is an important cue in this task, providing listeners with information about the speaker's next referent (Hanna & Brennan, 2007) and offering speakers some indication about whether listeners correctly resolved their references (Clark & Krych, 2004). However, investigating listener gaze in response to spoken referring expression and, importantly, the benefit of listener gaze for the speaker, is non-trivial and requires a dynamic setting. Specifically, it requires s a shared task, a sufficiently complex environment, the systematic production of referring expressions and an appropriate reaction to listener gaze.

We present a new technique with which we successfully demonstrate that monitoring listener gaze and giving appropriate feedback enhances reference resolution by the listener. This technique employs a visually-situated, interactive natural language generation (NLG) system that exploits real-time user gaze. Users must following directional instructions, including pressing a number of buttons in the 3D environment that are identified using referring expression generated by the system, in order to find a trophy (see GIVE; Koller et al., 2010). Users' eye movements are remotely monitored for signs of referential success by mapping them to objects in the virtual environment. Gaze to the intended referent during or shortly after a referring expression is taken as evidence of successful understanding and elicits positive feedback; by contrast, gaze to other objects triggers negative feedback.

We compare this eye movement-based strategy of giving feedback with a system that generates feedback based on visibility of objects on the screen and the user's movements towards an object, as well as with a system that generates no such feedback. Performance measures reveal that the eye-movement based feedback leads to significantly more successful button presses than both the movement-based strategy and the no-feedback strategy. Further, confusion – as indicated by the overall number of requests for help – is significantly lower for eye movement-based feedback than for the two other strategies. This suggests that listener gaze between a referring expression and the intended button press indeed indicates how a listener resolved the

expression and that giving appropriate feedback can encourage or correct the listener for more efficient grounding of references.

Finally, user eye movements further reveal that the speaker's feedback to listener gaze (in contrast to movement-based feedback) generally increases looks towards all potential referents. Given that post-experiment questionnaires suggest that users did not take notice of being eye-tracked, we consider this to show that eye-movement based feedback implicitly increases visual attention to all potential targets. In conclusion, this study demonstrates that referential gaze findings from the visual world paradigm do appear to scale to dynamic and task-centered environments, and further suggest that listener gaze can be used in real-time to improve situated spoken language interaction.

References

Hanna, J. and Brennan, S. (2007) Speakers'eye gaze disambiguates referring expressions early during face-to-face conversation. *Journal of Memory and Language*, 57, 596-615.

Clark, H.H. and Krych, M.A. (2004). Speaking while monitoring addressees for understanding. *Journal of Memory and Language*, 50(1), 62-81.

Koller, A., Striegnitz, K., Byron, D., Cassell, J., Dale, R., Moore, J., et al. (2010). The First Challenge on Generating Instructions in Virtual Environments. In E. Krahmer & M. Theune (Eds.), Empirical Methods in Natural Language Generation (pp. 337–361). Springer.

IDENTIFYING INSTANCES OF PROCESSING EFFORT IN TRANSLATION THROUGH HEAT MAPS: an eye-tracking study using multiple input sources

Fabio ALVES[1], *José Luiz GONÇALVES*[2], *Karina SZPAK*[1]
(1) FEDERAL UNIVERSITY OF MINAS GERAIS (UFMG), Av. Antonio Carlos 6627, Belo Horizonte/MG, 31.270-901, Brazil
(2) FEDERAL UNIVERSITY OF OURO PRETO (UFOP), Rua do Seminário, S/N, Mariana/MG, 35.420-000, Brazil
fabio-alves@ufmg.br, zeluizvr@ichs.ufop.br, kszpak@ufmg.br

ABSTRACT

Drawing on the seminal work of Just and Carpenter (1980), eye fixations have been used extensively to analyse instances of processing effort in studies of reading and writing processes. More recently, eye tracking has also been applied to experimental studies in translation process research (Jakobsen and Jensen 2008, Pavlović and Jensen 2009, Alves, Pagano and Silva 2009, Hvelplund 2011, Carl and Kay 2011, Carl and Dragsted 2012, among others). In most of these works, eye-tracking data have provided input for quantitative analyses of fixation count and duration in areas of interest in source and target texts. From a linguistic perspective, however, studies using eye-tracking data are considered rather complex since eye fixations tend to vary considerably among subjects. This paper attempts to tackle this issue by proposing a methodological approach that uses overlapped heat maps of different subjects to select and analyse translation problems. The results yield relevant findings for eye-tracking research in translation.

KEYWORDS: translation process research, eye-tracking research, eye-mind assumption, processing effort in translation, micro/macro translation units.

1 Introduction

According to Hvelplund (2011), the allocation of cognitive resources in translation is essentially an information-processing task and research using eye-tracking data as indicators of cognitive processing (Just and Carpenter 1980, Rayner 1998, Duchowski 2007) rests on the overall assumption that eye-tracking data can be interpreted as correlates of on-going cognitive processing of source and/or target texts. Building on Just and Carpenter's (1980) seminal work, analyses based on the eye-mind assumption suggest that eye fixations can be used as a window into instances of effortful cognitive processing. In more recent years, eye tracking has been used in translation process research to try to locate instances of effortful processing in translation. The works of Jakobsen and Jensen (2008), Pavlović and Jensen (2009), Alves, Pagano and Silva (2009), Alves, Pagano, Neumann, Steiner and Hansen-Schirra (2010), Hvelplund (2011), Carl and Kay (2011), and Carl and Dragsted (2012), among others, have shown that eye fixations differ in areas of interest (AOIs) found in source and/or target texts and, thus, suggest interesting implications in terms of reading/writing for translation.

Jakobsen and Jensen (2008) examined differences in reading for different purposes, namely reading for understanding, for translating, for sight translation and for written translation. Their results indicate that, as measured in terms of fixation duration, translators allocate more cognitive effort to target text (TT) processing rather than to correlated instances in source texts (ST). The results of Jakobsen and Jensen suggest that there is some evidence, although preliminary, that TT processing requires more cognitive effort than ST processing.

Pavlović and Jensen's (2009) investigated directionality in translation by observing the performance of professional and novice translators. They employed three eye-movement indicators, namely, total gaze time, fixation duration during ST and TT processing, and pupil dilation, to measure cognitive effort. Corroborating Jakobsen and Jensen's (2008) results, Pavlović and Jensen have also shown that TT processing requires more cognitive effort than ST processing and that ST comprehension and TT production are two processes which differ in terms of the cognitive effort.

The studies reported above used relatively small samples of eye-tracking data and, therefore, their statistical analyses are based on very small populations. As a word of caution, Jakobsen and Jensen (2008: 108) point out that "with such a small sample, any free variable can cause havoc in the data". More recent studies have thus tried to use larger population samples to increase the statistical significance of their results.

Hvelplund (2011), for instance, looked at differences between professional and novice translators and found that cognitive effort was higher for the latter than for the former group during ST and TT processing. Hvelplund builds on the concept of attention units (AU) to measure fixation duration and pupil dilation to gain insights into the allocation of cognitive effort in translation. His results indicate that professional translators rely more on automatic processing than novice translators. The results also show that switching attention between different types of cognitive processes is more demanding for novice translators than for professionals.

Carl and Kay (2011) also analysed shifts of attention with respect to the segment being processed and segments that lie ahead. They report that a production pause of more than 1000ms in text production is likely to represent a shift of attention towards another segment. Their results have shown that professional translators are capable of typing a translation while already reading ahead in the ST, whereas novice translators often resort to a sequential mode and can only carry out one activity at the same time, thus alternating between actions related to reading and writing.

Carl and Dragsted (2012) have used eye-tracking data to investigate differences between copying and translations tasks. They have shown that translators often resort to sequential reading and writing patterns that seem to be triggered through TT production problems. Carl and Dragsted found evidence of more processing effort during translation than during copying tasks. This indicates more sequential reading/writing processes in translation, whereas parallel reading and writing activities appear to be more prevalent during copying tasks.

In these recent works, eye-tracking data have been studied with a focus on statistical significance and have provided relevant insights into how the translation process unfolds in terms of the allocation of processing effort. However, as Alves, Pagano and Silva (2009) have shown, a fine-grained linguistic analysis of translation problems may also shed light onto relevant aspects of cognitive processing in translation. They claim that such analyses require an account provided by a pertinent linguistic theory. This point has also been addressed by Alves, Pagano, Neumann, Steiner and Hansen-Schirra (2010) in their analysis of micro/macro translation units (cf. Alves and Vale 2009). Alves and Gonçalves (forthcoming) have drawn on Relevance Theory (Sperber and Wilson 1986/1995) and its effort/effect relation to offer an insightful alternative for such fine-grained linguistic analysis by investigating the allocation of effort from a relevance-theoretic perspective. However, Alves and Gonçalves only analysed key-logged data although eye-tracking data had also been collected in their experimental design.

From a linguistic perspective, studies using eye-tracking data are still incipient and considered rather complex since eye fixations tend to vary considerably among subjects. In this paper, we attempt to fill this gap by using eye-tracking data to supplement Alves and Gonçalves's (forthcoming) analyses of macro translation units and propose a methodological framework that extracts individually gaze-relevant data and combines them into sets of overlapped heat maps which highlight instances where processing effort is greater for a given number of subjects. We claim that this methodological approach can offer an alternative to carry out linguistic analyses of eye-tracking data in translation process research.

2 Theoretical underpinnings

Relevance Theory (Sperber and Wilson 1986/1995) has been applied to the study of processing effort in translation, mainly by using the relevance-theoretic concepts of conceptual and procedural encodings proposed by Blakemore (2002) in order to identify a relation between processing effort and cognitive effect.

In relevance-theoretic terms, the function of conceptual expressions (i.e., open lexical categories, such as nouns, adjectives and verbs) is to convey conceptual meaning which is propositionally extendable and contributes to expanding the inferential processing of an utterance, whereas the function of procedural expressions is to activate domain-specific cognitive procedures (i.e., morph-syntactic constraints in utterance processing) and contributes to constraining the inferential processing of these same utterances. Relevance Theory assumes that the conceptual-procedural distinction guides inferential processing. And since most content words also carry some procedural meaning (Wilson 2011), therefore, processing effort in translation should concentrate more on instances of procedural than conceptual encodings.

The studies of Alves (2007) and Alves and Gonçalves (2003) have show there is a relation between processing effort and cognitive effect in translation and also that the conceptual-procedural distinction plays a role in such processes. However, these were small-scale studies that only offered qualitative results. Using a larger population, Alves and Gonçalves's (forthcoming) have tried to build on the previous relevance-theoretic findings and corroborate them by means of statistical analyses. They have used key-logged data to map instances of conceptual and procedural encodings onto micro/macro translation units (cf. Alves and Vale 2009, 2011). Their results show that procedural encodings demand more processing effort both in direct and inverse translation tasks.

According to Alves and Vale (2011: 107), a micro translation unit (TU) is defined as "[...] the flow of continuous target text production – which may incorporate the continuous reading of source and target text segments – separated by pauses during the translation process as registered by key-logging and/or eye-tracking software. It can be correlated to a source text segment that attracts the translator's focus of attention at a given moment." A macro TU, on the other hand, is "[...] defined as a collection of micro TUs that comprises all the interim text productions that follow the translator's focus on the same ST segment from the first tentative rendering to the final output that appears in the TT." Alves and Vale classify macro TUs with editing procedures taking place only in the drafting phase as P1. Those macro TUs that are produced once in the drafting phase and changed only in the revision phase are classified as P2. Finally, those macro TUs that undergo editing procedures both during drafting and revision are classified as P3. Alves and Gonçalves's (forthcoming) have broadened Alves and Vale's (2011) taxonomy to include a P0 unit, corresponding to micro TUs that do not undergo any editing at all and, therefore, are also considered macro TUs for annotation purposes.

In their attempt to map instances of conceptual and procedural encodings onto translation process data, Alves and Gonçalves's (forthcoming) have also annotated more detailed editing procedures inside each macro TU. Their distinctions were based on two types of annotation parameters: (a) the level of linguistic complexity in an editing procedure; and (b) the distance between this change and the respective initial micro TU. Alves and Gonçalves assumed that both parameters are related to processing effort and that the higher the linguistic complexity involved in the editing procedure and the farther it is from the respective initial micro TU, the greater the processing effort required.

The results of Alves and Gonçalves's (forthcoming) suggest that the allocation of cognitive resources in translation can be illustrated as P0>P1>P3>P2. Drawing on relevance-theoretic assumptions, the authors argue that subjects concentrate editing procedures within or very close to the respective initial micro TU and systematically attempt to reduce processing effort in order to optimize the resources in their cognitive environments. If they postpone the solution to a problem, or only fully realize this problem later on, the required processing effort needed to re-activate relevant information will be counter-productive in terms of cognitive processing economy. This is consistent with the relevance-theoretic framework, since additional processing effort diminishes the relevance of the cognitive effects.

Alves and Gonçalves have also found that the total number of occurrences for conceptual and procedural encoding editing procedures is highest in P1, followed by P3. They assume that this can be interpreted in terms of allocation of processing effort to phases in the translation process, indicating where this effort is greater. In P1, subjects interrupt the cognitive flow to deal with more immediate processing problems. In P3, however, problem solving is postponed to the end-revision phase. Their results point to prevalence of processing effort for procedural encodings in absolute terms, particularly in P1 and P3 where processing effort seems to be concentrated.

An interesting question that emerges from the study of Alves and Gonçalves's (forthcoming) is whether an analysis of eye-tracking data from the same subjects would also corroborate the assumption that eye fixations should be higher and longer in instances of P1 and P3. It would also be interesting to find out if the number of eye fixations would be higher in instances of procedural encodings. However, this would be extremely time-consuming if the whole set of data were to be analysed. In this paper, we propose a methodology to analyse selected instances of translation problems on the basis of overlapped heat maps to provide a fine-grained analysis on the basis of a smaller but yet relevant set of data.

3 Methodology

Eight Brazilian translators with at least five years of professional experience were asked to translate two sets of comparable STs, each set comprising a text to be translated from English (L2) into Portuguese (L1) – direct translation (DT) – and another text to be rendered from Portuguese (L1) into English (L2) – inverse translation (IT). The first set consisted of abstracts of approximately 250 words each, one in English and the other one in Portuguese, both dealing with the topic of sickle cell disease. The second set of STs of approximately 200 words each consisted of popular science texts, namely an English ST about the physics of crumpling paper and a Portuguese ST about the properties of an electronic tongue. For the translation of the first set of STs translators had free access to the Internet and were allowed to use different sources of documentation. Task order was randomized in order to control for a likely facilitating effect. For the translation of the second set of STs, translators were allowed to use only one electronic dictionary (Babylon). Subjects were instructed by a brief with a detailed description of the task at hand and no time pressure was applied.

The overall goal was to investigate whether subject's performance differed in terms of processing conceptual and procedural encodings while performing a DT and an IT task. As explained in the theoretical section, the same data set was analysed by Alves and Gonçalves (forthcoming) to investigate processing effort in translation from a relevance-theoretic perspective. Their results showed that instances of procedural encodings require more processing effort than cases of conceptual encodings. However, Alves and Gonçalves only analysed key-logged data. As the replication of their methodology using eye-tracking data would be extremely time consuming for the whole data set, we propose here a methodological alternative that focuses on a smaller set of selected examples to see if they yield similar results in relevance-theoretic terms.

3.1 Internal and external support as input for eye-tracking data

A major methodological problem in the analysis of conceptual and procedural encodings would be the impact of external support in the complete data set. During task execution, subjects often deviate their gaze from the computer screen or open other windows to look up dictionary entries and/or perform web searches. These actions are an integral part of the translation process but are of no particular interest for the investigation of conceptual and procedural encodings. Therefore, data related to external support had to be filtered out from data related to internal support, i.e, those instances when translators effectively dealt with the linguistic processing of conceptual and procedural encodings.

3.1.1 Filtering out external support from eye-tracking data

As a first step into that direction, the eye-tracking recordings from Jane, Cycy, Adam, Jim, Will, Mona, Tess, and Rui, the fictitious names for the 8 professional translators who volunteered as subjects, were screened using the software Tobii Studio. Altogether there were 32 recordings, 8 from each DT or IT task. As shown in Figure 1, each recording was edited to create a set of scenes which only contained eye-tracking data directly related to internal support. In other words, the filtered data did not show instances of consultations or gaze deviations from the screen and provided access to the linguistic processing of instances of conceptual and procedural encodings.

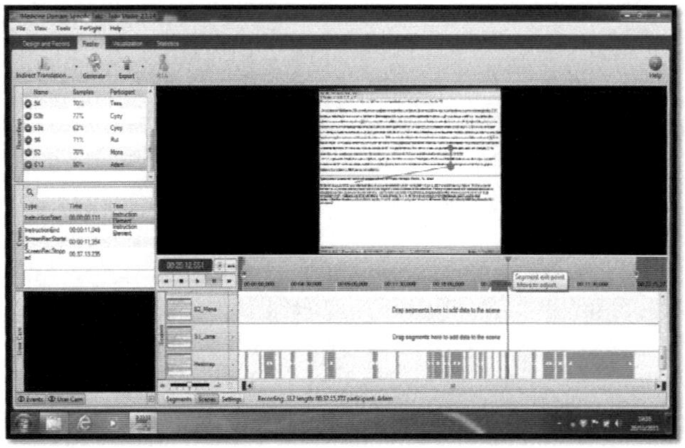

FIGURE 1 – preparation of individual eye-tracking data with internal support only

Using the Tobii Studio replay mode, we selected those stretches of the translation process which related to internal support only. This can be seen in the centre of Figure 1. On the bottom part of the screen, one can visualize the process time line shown in the selection bar. One can click on the white parts of the cursor and drag the mouse to create the desired scenes which are then shown in red and stored by the software. The set of scenes from each subject can be retrieved by clicking on the icon *scenes* on the bottom part of the computer screen. As a second step, sets of scenes of internal support from each subject were combined to create a set of scenes from the eight subjects for each of the four translation tasks. Thus, the Tobii Studio *Add Selection to Scene* tool was used to group eye-tracking data of all eight subjects and generate four sets of eye-tracking data, two pertaining DT tasks (DT_1 and DT_2) and two others related to IT tasks (IT_1 and IT_2).

3.2 Extracting heat maps

The creation of individual and group scenes related to internal support aimed at identifying through heat maps those areas of STs and TTs where eye fixations were longer. We expected subjects to show idiosyncratic gaze patterns and, therefore, heat maps would differ among them. However, by overlapping eight correlated sets of scenes, we were able to generate heat maps which are representative of each task in terms of eye fixations. Heat maps provided by Tobii Studio show both fixation count and fixation duration from a graphic perspective according to visual activity. Areas with higher fixation count and longer duration are shown in red and shades become orange, yellow or green as visual activity decreases in intensity. Such activities are easily identified in both ST and TT areas. Instances where those fixations were longer were then considered to be potential candidates for translation problems that were cognitively relevant for all subjects in terms of processing effort. For the purposes of this paper, we would argue that fixation count is a reliable measure for assessing cognitive effort since there is a tendency for fixations to converge to an average duration when dealing with a great deal of occurrences.

3.2.1 Extracting individual heat maps

From the individual scene sets that had been created by filtered data of internal support only, heat maps were generated for each subject. Using the Tobii Studio visualization mode, we selected the desired scenes and clicked on the heat map icon to generate them automatically. Figure 2 shows individual heat maps for the data set 1, comprising DT task 1 and DT task 2 while Figure 3 displays the individual heat maps for data set 2, comprising IT task 1 and IT task 2.

Figures 2 and 3 show idiosyncratic gaze patterns. One notices that red areas, where eye fixations are longer, appear at disparate places in data sets 1 and 2, respectively the DT and IT tasks. The upper part of each screen shot relates to the ST area of interest (AOI) whereas the lower part of each screen shot refers to the TT AOI. In some screen shots one notices a white area separating these two blocks, clearly identifying gaze activity pertaining to STs and TTs.

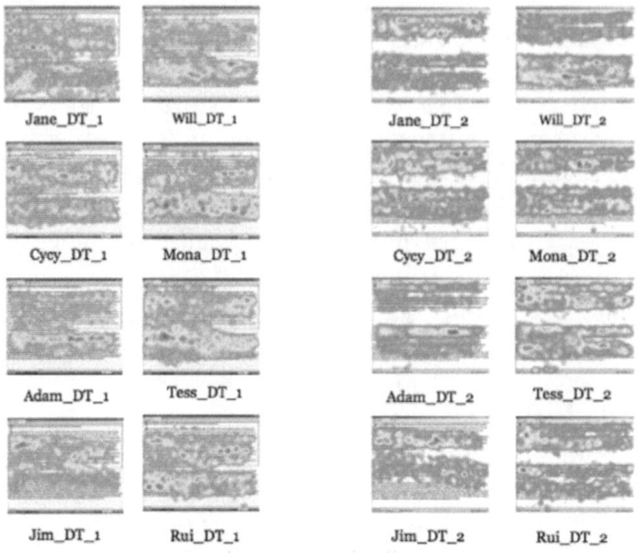

FIGURE 2 – Individual heat maps for data set 1.

The same procedure was repeated for the filtered data related to the execution of IT tasks. Figure 3 shows individual heat maps for the data set 2, comprising IT task 1 and IT task 2.

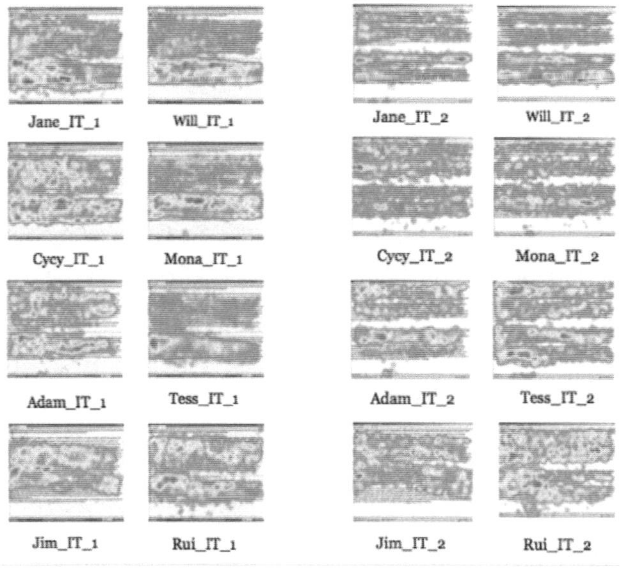

FIGURE 3 – individual heat maps for data set 2.

3.2.2 Extracting overlapped heat maps

A methodological alternative to avoid the undesired impact of idiosyncratic patterns is to overlap the eight individual heat maps for each of the four translation tasks. Using the Tobii Studio *Add Selection to Scene* tool, used to group eye-tracking data, it is possible to generate heat maps which show where eye fixations are longer for all the eight subjects together. These red areas are then considered potential candidates for translation problems which are cognitively relevant in terms of processing effort for the eight subjects on the whole.

Figure 4 shows heat maps for the data set 1, comprising DT tasks 1 and 2. In both tasks eye fixations are longer at the beginning of the English STs and on the first paragraph of the TT area which corresponds to the rendering of the translation into Portuguese. In our approach, we are not particularly concerned whether fixations are longer in ST or TT AOIs. Our interest lies explicitly on the linguistic encodings related to areas of stronger visual activity and to the features they convey.

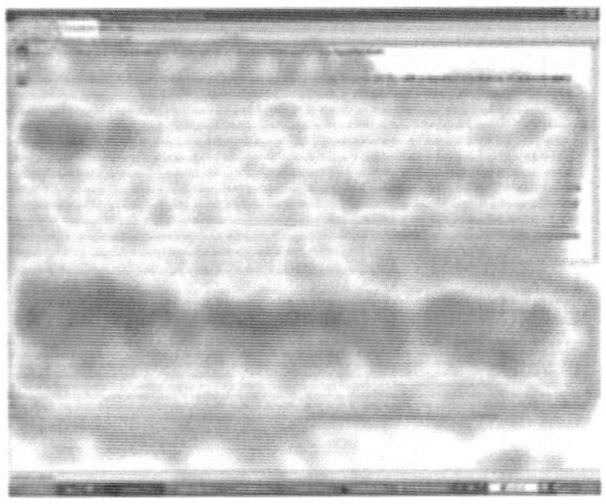

DT_1
All Subjects

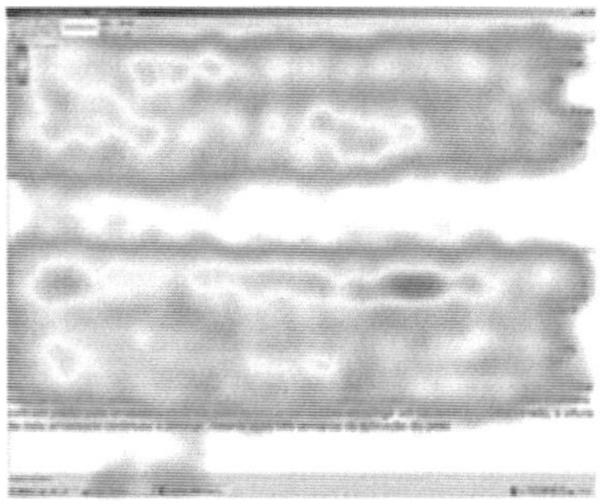

DT_2
All Subjects

FIGURE 4 – overlapped heat maps for DT – data sets 1 and 2.

Looking at the heat maps, one notices that some parts at the bottom of TT in DT_2 seem uncovered. It is important to point out that this is not related to eye-tracking data quality. It happens because, when heat maps are overlapped, the generated image shows the occurrences of all fixations statically. Individual heat maps displayed in Figures 2 and 3 show that such areas were indeed covered. The overlapped heat maps for TTs serve as an approximate indicator of the common region for the identification of problems while the translations were being drafted. Complementarily, the ST heat maps indicate the common problems among the eight subjects with respect to their reading patterns.

Figure 5 shows heat maps for the data set 2, comprising IT tasks 1 and 2. Similar to what was illustrated by Figure 4, eye fixations are longer at the beginning of the STs and on the first paragraph of each TT area which corresponds to the rendering of the translation into English. As for DT tasks, the overlapped heat maps for TTs serve as an approximate indicator of the common region for the identification of problems while the ST heat maps indicate the common problems with respect to the subjects' reading patterns.

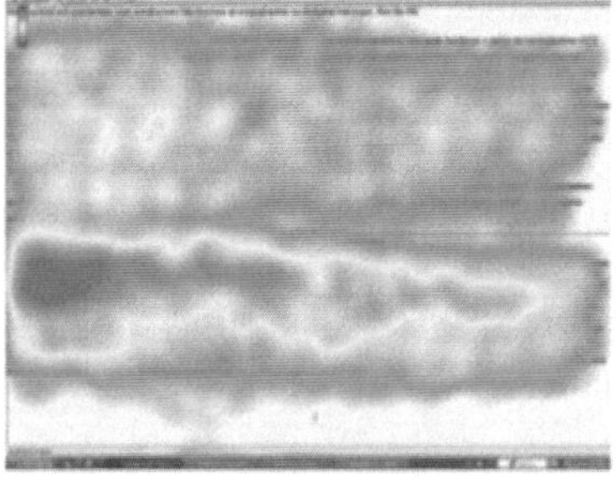

IT_1
All Subjects

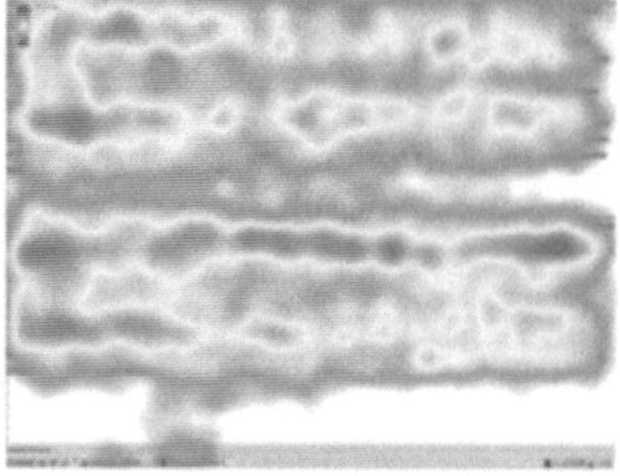

IT_2
All Subjects

FIGURE 5 – complete heat maps for IT – data sets 1 and 2.

In Figures 4 and 5, the heat maps are meant to illustrate how we have chosen the excerpts to be analyzed. The aim is not necessarily to show precisely the respective passages in the text, but rather to illustrate the inductive methodology applied in the paper in order to identify the problems under scrutiny.

Analysing the complete set of heat maps for DT and IT data sets 1 and 2, we notice that what had been observed for Figure 4 also applies to Figure 5. In both tasks eye fixations are long at the beginning of the STs and even longer on the first paragraph of each TT area which corresponds to the rendering of translation into English. Other areas of interest with higher visual activity are also found in the middle of the STs for DT and IT tasks and appear as pontential candidates for equally relevant translation problems in terms of processing effort.

3.3 Identifying potential translation problems through heat maps

Our next methodological step was to create areas of interest (AOI) for the selected instances with higher visual activity in order to extract statistically relevant information using the AOI Tool provided by Tobii Studio. Selecting the *Statistics* tab in the software, we can activate the desired metrics to obtain measures for fixation count, fixation duration, percentage of fixations, number of visits, etc.), and generate tables and graphics automatically.

We assume that there is no visual heat dispersion in the data. Tobii records and displays eye movements by using the center of the pupil and infrared to create corneal reflections that are tracked one or two degrees of the visual angle, known as foveal vision. The vector between the pupil center and the corneal reflections provide the right point of the gaze being tracked. Before data collection we carried out a calibration procedure for all subjects. Therefore, we eliminated the likelihood of visual dispersion in the data.

3.3.1 Potential translation problems for DT and IT

The selected areas in the heat maps displayed in Figures 4 and 5 point to interesting examples and suggest that they are considered to be complex issues by the majority of subjects.

This inductive approach offers a methodological solution for data extraction to be used in a more refined linguistic analysis. For the DT tasks, the first set of problems, located in the beginning of the English STs, corresponds to the title (see example 1) in DT_1 and to the first clause in DT_2 (see example 2).

(1) Coagulation activation and inflammation in sickle cell disease-associated pulmonary hypertension

(2) Crumpling a sheet of paper [...]

The second set of problems, located in the middle of the English STs, corresponds to the noun phrases shown in (3) for DT_1 and in (4) for DT_2.

(3) chronic fibrotic pulmonary parenchymal damage [...]

(4) a mass of conical points connected by curved ridges [...]

For the IT tasks, the third set of problems was located in the beginning of the Portuguese STs and corresponds to the title (see example 5) in IT_1, quite similar to the occurrence of (1) in DT_1, and to the first clause in IT_2 (see example 6), also similar to the occurrence of (2) in DT_2.

(5) Hidroxiuréia em pacientes com síndromes falciformes acompanhados no Hospital Hemope, Recife-PE [...]

(6) Avaliar um bom café [...]

Finally, last set of problems in the IT tasks was located in the middle of the Portuguese STs and corresponds to noun phrases in IT_1 and in IT_2 (see example 7 and 8).

(7) leucemia mielóide crônica e policitemia vera [...]

(8) uma camada fina de polímeros condutores [...]

One can observe a series of similarities for the problems selected in both DT and IT tasks. Problems (1) and (5) refer to the title of the STs and had, respectively, 11 and 12 words. They dealt with the same terminological problem (anemia falciforme/*sickle cell disease*). (1) and (5) are both complex noun phrases that seem to demand a lot of processing effort for their renderings.

One can also observe that (2) and (6) share similarities with (1) and (5). Like them, (2), the first clause in the English ST, is a verbal phrase that functions as a title, whereas (6) is an infinitive clause which also has the same function. Problems (2) and (6) have 5 and 4 words respectively, a relation they share with (1) and (5) which, with 11 and 12 words, also showed a similar pattern in terms of number of words. Problems (4) in DT_1, (5) in DT_2, (7) in IT_1 and (8) in IT_2 constitute a second set of translation problems with a middle location in the respective STs. Their extension ranges from 5 to 9 words. They are all noun phrases, (3) and (7) being related to the medical domain, whereas (4) and (8) belong to the domain of physics. In our methodological approach, the eight selected problems are deemed to be representative items for a linguistic analysis since they deal with conceptual and procedural encodings mapped onto micro/macro translation units.

In the next section, we analyse the data based on Alves and Gonçalves's (forthcoming) taxonomy to see if the results of eye-tracking data corroborate the findings obtained through the analysis of key-logged data. If they do, this would validate the use of smaller data sets of eye-tracking data selected for a fine-grained linguistic analysis.

4 Analysis and discussion

Our analysis builds on the results of Alves and Gonçalves (forthcoming) for key-logged data and compares them with the number of eye fixations for the selected AOIs that were analysed manually with respect to the type of macro TUs (P0, P1, P2, P3) and the type of linguistic editing procedure (t = typos, c = conclusion of a lexical item, l = lexical change, m = morph-syntactic change, p = changes at phrase level). The analysis focuses on the number of occurrences in STs and TTs in both DT and IT tasks. As shown in Alves, Pagano and Silva (2009) and in Alves and Gonçalves (forthcoming), directionality was not an intervening factor in the experimental design. Therefore, the number of fixations was counted for all tasks together irrespective of directionality. Building on Alves and Gonçalves (forthcoming), we decided to count conceptual encodings as the sums of [l+p] because each instance of [p] includes at least one instance of conceptual encoding. We have also decided to count procedural encoding as the sums of [m+p] because each instance of [p] also includes at least one instance of procedural encoding.

In Alves and Gonçalves (forthcoming), there were 504 occurrences of P0 macro TUs, followed by 410 occurrences of P1, 119 occurrences of P3 and, finally, 47 occurrences of P2 macro TUs. In other words, P0>P1>P3>P2; a progression which was interpreted as a sign of cognitive complexity and higher processing effort in translation.

Table 1 shows the absolute and relative numbers of eye fixations in the selected AOIs containing the eight examples described in the previous section. As stated in the methodology, we assume that these AOIs are relevant indicators of cognitive complexity and higher processing effort and show similar patterns found for key-logged data, namely, P0>P1>P3>P2 for both ST and TT AOIs, and for the complete set of data on the whole.

Type of Macro TU	P0	P1	P2	P3
Source Text (ST)	1800 (64.9%)	1387 (51.2%)	101 (22.0%)	129 (16.9%)
Target Text (TT)	973 (35.1%)	1324 (48.8%)	358 (78.0%)	635 (83.1%)
TOTAL	2773	2711	459	764

TABLE 1 – Number of eye fixations in macro TUs in ST and TT AOIs

Alves and Gonçalves (forthcoming) consider P0 as an indicator of low difficulty as processing effort unfolds without interruption in the flow of TT production. With 2773 fixation counts, P0 shows the highest number of eye fixations, namely 64.9% of counts (1800) in the ST AOI in comparison with the 35.1% of counts (973) in the TT AOI, i.e., nearly twice more eye fixations in the ST than in the TT. For P1 macro TUs, which also occur very close to the cognitive flow of TT production, the results in Table 1 show a very similar number of fixations (1387/1324) with 51.2% of them occurring in ST AOI and 48.4% in the TT AOI. When compared to the number of eye fixations for P0 macro TUs, we notice a decrease in the number of fixations in the ST from 64.9% down to 51.2%, and an increase in the number of fixations in the TT, from 35.1% up to 48.4%.

Considering that P1 macro TUs account mainly for online revisions carried out in the sequential flow of cognitive processing, a balanced focus of attention in eye fixations between ST and TT suggests that P1 macro TUs are cognitively more demanding that P0 macro TUs. On the other hand, the patterns for P2 and P3 macro TUs show a completely different picture. The number of P3 macro TUs (764) is significantly higher than the number of P2 macro TUs (459). Both P2 and P3 also show another congruent pattern with a much higher number of eye fixations occurring in the TT AOI. Bearing in mind that P3 is cognitively more demanding than P2, it is interesting to observe that there are over five times more eye fixations in the TT AOI for P3 than in the ST AOI (129/635), and over three times more eye fixations in the TT AOI for P2 than in the ST AOI (101/358).

All these results are statistically significant when the Student t-test is applied. They provide evidence that subjects tend to concentrate their focus of attention on the ST AOI when renderings unfold in the cognitive flow of TT production without interruption. Results also show a balanced focus of attention with alternations between ST and TT AOIs in cases of P1 macro TUs. And, as the translation process become more demanding in terms of cognitive complexity, subjects tend to focus their gaze on the TT AOI for both P2 and P3 macro TUs.

These results corroborate the findings of Alves and Gonçalves (forthcoming), for key-logged data. They are also in line with Carl and Dragsted (2012) when the authors claim that problem solving in translation seem to be triggered through TT production problems. In their analysis of key-logged data, Alves and Gonçalves (forthcoming) have also shown that, as far as the type of linguistic encoding is concerned, processing effort in translation is greater for procedural encodings than for conceptual encodings. Table 2 displays the number of eye fixations for typos [t], completion of lexical items [c], changes of lexical items [l], editing of a morph-syntactic nature [m], and modifications on the phrase level [p] in the selected AOIs. As shown in Alves and Gonçalves (forthcoming), encodings of [t] and [c] types tend to occur in the flow of TT production and are more prevalent in P1 macro TUs. It is interesting to observe that, with 1637 counts, [t] has the highest number of eye fixations in the whole set of data whereas, with 470 counts, [c] shows the lowest number of fixations. Nevertheless, both [t] and [c] show a somewhat balanced pattern in the number of eye fixations with, respectively, 846 and 791 counts in ST and TT AOIs for [t] and 224 and 246 counts in ST and TT AOIs for [c].

Type of Encoding	t	c	l	m	p
Source Text (ST)	846 (51.7%)	224 (47.7%)	134 (27.2%)	254 (36.1%)	159 (25.2%)
Target Text (TT)	791 (48.3%)	246 (52.3%)	359 (72.8%)	449 (63.3%)	472 (74.8%)
TOTAL	1637	470	493	703	631

TABLE 2 – Number of eye fixations for types of encodings in ST and TT AOIs

This balanced distribution can be interpreted as evidence that [t] and [c] are actions not necessarily related to the translation process per se but rather entail typing activities such as correcting typing mistakes or finishing typing a word after looking for the right key on the keyboard. Since most subjects were not touch typists, this type of action is expected and should be filtered out from an analysis of processing effort. The pattern is altogether different when [l], [m], and [p] editing procedures are analysed.

Table 2 shows that in terms of fixation counts [m]>[p]>[l] in ST and TT AOIs. This result is statistically significant when the Student t-test is applied. Following Alves and Gonçalves (forthcoming), if [l]+[p] and [m]+[p] are grouped together, the number of eye fixations confirm the claim that processing effort in translation is higher in instances of procedural encodings.

Conclusions and perspectives

The picture emerging from our analyses is manifold. The results point to the validity of the proposed methodology for the selection of translation problems that seem to be relevant for a fine grained linguistic analysis of eye-tracking data. The selected AOIs have proved to be a valid choice which not only confirmed the findings of Alves and Gonçalves's (forthcoming) key-logging analysis for the same set of data, but also corroborated Carl and Dragted's (2012) claim that problem solving in translation is TT driven.

This can be shown by the different patterns of eye fixations for P0, P1, P2 and P3 macro TUs, whereas P1 shows a balanced distribution in the number of eye fixations in ST and TT AOIs and P2 and P3 clearly indicate that eye fixations are more prevalent in the TT AOIs with an even much higher difference when P3 macro TUs are compared with P2 macro TUs. The number of eye fixations observed in the analysis of linguistic encodings also reveals striking differences between two groups of editing procedures, with [t] and [c] showing a completely different picture from [l], [m], and [p]. From a relevance-theoretic perspective these differences point to instances where effortful TT production is greater and show that procedural encodings require more processing effort than conceptual encodings.

References

Alves, F., editor (2003). *Triangulating Translation: Perspectives in Process-Oriented Research.* John Benjamins, Amsterdam.

Alves, F. (2007). Cognitive Effort and Contextual Effect in Translation: a Relevance-theoretic Approach. *Journal of Translation Studies* 10(1):18–35.

Alves, F. and Gonçalves, J. L. (2003). A Relevance Theory Approach to the Investigation of Inferential Processes in Translation. In (Alves, 2003), pages 3–24.

Alves, F. and Gonçalves, J. L. (forthcoming). Investigating the conceptual-procedural distinction in the translation process: a relevance-theoretic analysis of micro and macro translation units. To appear in *Target* 25(1).

Alves, F., Pagano, A., Neumann, S., Steiner, E. and Hansen-Schirra, S. (2010). Translation units and grammatical shifts: towards an integration of product and process-based translation research. In (Shreve and Angelone, 2010), pages 109–142.

Alves, F., Pagano, A. and Silva, I.A.L. (2009). A new window on translators' cognitive activity: methodological issues in the combined use of eye tracking, key logging and retrospective protocols. In (Mees el al, 2009), pages 267–292.

Alves, F. and Vale, D. (2009). Probing the unit of translation in time: aspects of the design and development of a web application for storing, annotating, and querying translation process data. *Across Languages and Cultures* 10(2):251–273.

Alves, F. and Vale, D. (2011). On drafting and revision in translation: a corpus linguistics oriented analysis of translation process data. *TC3 Translation: Corpora, Computation, and Cognition* 1(1):105–122.

Carl, M. and Kay, M. (2011). Gazing and Typing Activities during Translation: A Comparative Study of Translation Units of Professional and Student Translators. *Meta: Journal des Traducteurs* 56(4):952–975.

Carl, M. and Dragsted, B. (2012). Inside the Monitor Model: Processes of Default and Challenged Translation Production. *Translation: Computation, Corpora, Cognition* 2(1):127–145.

Duchowski, A.T. (2007). *Eye Tracking Methodology: Theory and Practice.* Springer, London.

Göpferich, S., Jakobsen, A.L. and Mees. I.M., editors (2008). *Looking at Eyes: Eye-Tracking Studies of Reading and Translation Processing* (Copenhagen Studies in Language 36). Samfundslitteratur, Copenhagen.

Hvelplund, K.T.J. (2011). *Allocation of cognitive resources in translation: an eye-tracking and key-logging study.* Unpublished Ph.D. Thesis. Copenhagen Business School, Copenhagen.

Jakobsen, A.L. and Jensen K.T.H. (2008). Eye movement behaviour across four different types of reading task. In (Göpferich et al, 2008), pages 103–124.

Just, M.A. and Carpenter, P.A. (1980). A theory of reading: from eye fixations to comprehension. *Psychological Review* 87(4):329–354.

Mees, I., Alves, F. and Göpferich, S., editors (2009). *Methodology, Technology and Innovation in Translation Process Research: A Tribute to Arnt Lykke Jakobsen.* (Copenhagen Studies in Language 37). Samfundslitteratur, Copenhagen.

Pavlović, N. and Jensen, K.T.H. (2009). Eye tracking translation directionality. In (Pym and Perekrestenko, 2009), pages 101–119.

Pym, A. and Perekrestenko, A. editors (2009). *Translation Research Projects 2.* Universitat Rovira i Virgili, Tarragona.

Rayner, K. (1998). Eye movements in reading and information processing: 20 years of research. *Psychological Bulletin* 124:372–422.

Shreve, G. and Angelone, E., editors (2010). *Translation and Cognition.* John Benjamins, Amsterdam.

Sperber, D. and Wilson, D. (1986). *Relevance: Communication and Cognition.* Oxford: Blackwell. (Second edition 1995.)

Robustness and processing difficulty models. A pilot study for eye-tracking data on the *French Treebank*

Stéphane RAUZY   *Philippe BLACHE*
Aix-Marseille Université & CNRS
Laboratoire Parole & Langage
Aix-en-Provence, France
stephane.rauzy@lpl-aix.fr, philippe.blache@lpl-aix.fr

ABSTRACT
We present in this paper a robust method for predicting reading times. Robustness first comes from the conception of the difficulty model, which is based on a *morpho-syntactic surprisal* index. This metric is not only a good predictor, as shown in the paper, but also intrinsically robust (because relying on POS-tagging instead of parsing). Second, robustness also concerns data analysis: we propose to enlarge the scope of reading processing units by using syntactic chunks instead of words. As a result, words with null reading time do not need any special treatment or filtering. It appears that working at chunks scale smooths out the variability inherent to the different reader's strategy. The pilot study presented in this paper applies this technique to a new resource we have built, enriching a French treebank with eye-tracking data and difficulty prediction measures.

KEYWORDS: Linguistic complexity, difficulty models, morpho-syntactic surprisal, reading time prediction, chunks.

---

1 Introduction

Eye-tracking data are now often used in the study of language complexity (e.g. difficulty metrics evaluation) as well as finer syntactic studies (e.g. relative complexity of alternative constructions). However, only few resources exist, for a small number of languages. We describe in this paper a pilot study aiming at developing a high-level resource enriching a treebank with physiological data and complexity measures. This work have been done for French, with several objectives : (1) building a new large resource for French, freely available, associating syntactic information, eye-tracking data and difficulty prediction at different levels (tokens, chunks and phrases) (2) validating a difficulty model for French in the line of what has been done for other languages (Demberg and Keller, 2008), (Boston et al., 2008) relying on a robust surprisal index described in (Blache and Rauzy, 2011).

This pilot study, on top of building a new resource, had important side-effects. First, this work led us to examine carefully the question of *data analysis*. In particular, we found that working with larger units (syntactic chunks) instead of tokens makes it possible to take into consideration the entire set of data. In other words, it is not anymore necessary to eliminate data that are usually considered for different reasons as problematic (tokens ending lines, before punctuations, etc.). This result is important for several reasons. First, it avoids the use of truncated data (which is problematic in a statistical point of view). Second, it supports the hypothesis that chunks are not only functional, but can also be defined in linguistic terms by means of syntactic relation strength. Another interesting result is the influence of the syntactic parameter on the global model: we show that (morpho)syntax has modest impact in comparison with word frequency and word length. Finally, at the technical level, we have developed an entire experimental setup, facilitating data acquisition when using *Tobii* devices. Our environment proposes tools for the preparation of the experimental material (slide generation) as well as data post-processing (e.g. lines model detection).

2 Background

The study of language complexity first relies on theoretical difficulty models. Several proposals can be found in the literature, exploring the influence of different parameters on the parsing mechanism (Gibson, 1998, 2000), (Hawkins, 2001), (Vasishth, 2003). One important problem is the possibility to quantify the difficulty level: some metrics have been proposed such as *Dependency Locality Theory* (Gibson, 1998) which uses the number of new discourse referents in an integration region. Evaluating such models relies on the comparison of similar constructions, one being known to be more difficult than another (for example, object vs. subject relative clauses). Prototypical examples of such alternations are built and the model applied incrementally, estimating at each word the integration costs. Such models rely on high-level linguistic information, capable of bringing together syntactic and lexical semantic information, as well as integrating frequency information. In such cases, difficulty estimation is done manually, the validation applied only to few examples.

Recently, the development of probabilistic NLP techniques opened a new way in difficulty estimation. The idea consists in using the probability of the integration of a word into a partial parse as a predictor for human difficulty. The *Surprisal* index (Hale, 2001) implements this proposal: the mechanism consists in evaluating at each word the difference between probability of the set of trees before the word and that integrating the word. Several works such as (Demberg and Keller, 2008) have shown that *Surprisal* can be a predictor for reading time and, as a consequence, for language processing difficulty. The interest in these experiments is that, thanks to automatic difficulty evaluation, it becomes possible to work on larger amounts of data, offering the possibility to study language in more natural contexts.

We present in the remaining of this section an overview of different works addressing this question and propose an analysis of their characteristics, in particular with respect to the kind of data they use.

2.1 Experimental evaluations of complexity models

(Demberg and Keller, 2008) proposes an evaluation of two syntactic complexity theories (*DLT* and *Surprisal*) for the prediction of readers difficulty. Linear mixed effects models are experimented, taking into account non-syntactic predictors besides complexity measures. Such predictors are low-level variables known to have an impact on reading times[1]: word frequency, word length, position in the sentence (final words in the sentence are read faster). Oculomotor variables also have to be considered: fixation of a previous word, number of characters between two fixations, position of the fixation in the word. Higher level contextual variables are also proposed: forward transitional probability (probability of a word knowing the previous one) and backward transitional probability (probability of a word knowing the next one). As for the surprisal parameter, two different version have been used: one calculating surprisal taking into consideration the word forms, the other the POS tags. The experimental data rely on the English part of the Dundee corpus (Kennedy et al., 2003). This corpus comprises 51,502 tokens, from 20 newspaper articles (from *The Independent*). Eye-tracking data have been acquired for 10 subjects. Different eye-tracking measures are considered: *first fixation duration (FFD)* in a region, *first pass duration (FPD)* (total of all the fixations in a region when reading it for the first time) and *total reading time (TRD)* of a region (all the fixations, including those when going back into a region that has already been read).

In the experiment, (Demberg and Keller, 2008) eliminates from the original corpus several data: first and last tokens of each line, token followed by a punctuation, region of 4 words with no fixations and words with zero value for FFD and FPD . Finally, this experiment retains a total of 200,684 data points, which means 20,068 tokens read by 10 subjects.

The results of this study show that unlexicalized surprisal can predict reading times, whereas the lexicalized formulation does not. However, (Monsalve et al., 2012) pointed out recently that when using independent sentences, both lexicalized and unlexicalized surprisal measures are significant predictors of reading time (measures done with corpus of around 2,500 words and 54 participants).

These different studies focus on lexical and syntactic effects. In a complementary direction, (Pynte et al., 2009) analyzed the influence of superficial *lexical semantics* on fixation duration. (Mitchell et al., 2010) integrates this parameter into *Surprisal*. This work shows the effect of semantic costs in addition to syntactic surprisal for reading time prediction. It also addresses in a specific way the question of modeling: experimental studies usually use linear mixed effect models, including random effects (e.g. participants characteristics) and fixed ones (e.g. word frequency). In these approaches, many different parameters are brought together. As authors pointed out, the use of a unique measure for predicting complexity is preferable than a set of factors, not only for simplicity, but also because it is difficult to analyze the effective contribution of a factor: one can evaluate whether adding it into a model improves it fits, but cannot explain the reasons.

[1] See (Demberg and Keller, 2008) p.196 for a precise description.

2.2 Parameters and data

The different experiments have shown that *Surprisal* can play a significant role in a complexity model. All such models bring together different parameters at different levels: oculomotor (positions of the fixations), lexical (properties of the lexical items) and syntactic (contextual characteristics). Moreover, surprisal presents the advantage to be calculated for lexical items (taking into account the specific properties of each token, including co-occurrence) as well as POS, the last case being apparently more robust.

The complexity models in these different studies are linear mixed-effects and make use of many predictors. The following table recapitulates the main parameters used in the different studies[2]:

	Demberg08	Mitchell10	McDonald03	Monsalve12	Boston08	Roark09
Word length	+	+	+	+	+	+
Word freq.	+	+	+	+	+	+
Sentence position	+			+		
Word position				+		
Landing position	+	+	+			
Launch distance	+	+				
Previous word RT	+	+		+		
Lexicalized surp.	+			+	+	
Unlexicalized surp.	+			+		+
Bigram prob.		+	+		+	
Forward trans.	+		+	+		
Backward trans.	+		+	+		
Integration costs	+					
Lexical surp. entropy					+	
Synt supr. entropy					+	
Derivation steps					+	
Semantic		+				
Predictability			+		+	
Retrieval					+	

Arbitrarily, we distinguish in this table between low and high level predictors, the first usually being the baseline. As expected, word length and word frequency are used in all considered models, other predictors being less systematic. One can observe that the combinatory is very important and many different models have been experimented.

By another way, these experiments have shown the importance of input data. Until recently, studies on linguistic complexity was done on controlled material (artificially built sentences, out of context, small corpora). *Surprisal* relying on well-known NLP techniques, it offers the advantage to be applied to unrestricted corpora. (Demberg and Keller, 2008) evaluates this measure against a large corpus of newspaper articles, which constitutes an important step towards the treatment of *natural data* (even though the idea of contextualized material has been challenged by (Monsalve et al., 2012)). However, the main problem with the size of input data is that only few corpora with eye-tracking data are available. The Dundee corpus is, to the best of our knowledge, the only one with a reasonable size in a NLP perspective. Other existing corpora are much smaller, such as the *Embra* (McDonald and Shillcock, 2003) which comprises around 2,600 words. Another problem when dealing with large amount of data is the sensibility of the measures to parsers efficiency. No precise indication is given in these works, in spite of the fact that this constitutes a big issue (parsers F-scores being usually close to 85%).

A last feature shared by these different experiments lies in data cleaning. For different reasons, large part of the input material is excluded: position in the line, fixation duration, even in some

[2]For sake of place, these predictors are not described here. Their definition can be found in the corresponding papers.

cases morpho-syntactic category. Even though such pre-processing is usual in psycholinguistics, it constitutes a problem, in particular in terms of data analysis, as it will be explained later.

3 Experiment

As shown in the previous section, corpus used in the different experiments are very different in size and nature. (Demberg and Keller, 2008) explicitly focuses on naturalistic data. On the opposite, (Boston et al., 2008) relies on a very small corpus, but with large amount of subjects. The following table presents the main features of the different corpora. It mentions the number of token presented to the readers, the number of subjects participating to the experiment, the number of data points (roughly speaking fixation points) taken into account in the evaluation (after eliminating problematic data), the average number of tokens read by the subjects and taken into account after data filtering (data points are more or less the number of participants times the number of remaining tokens) and the experimental method.

	Tokens	Participants	Data points	Remaining tokens	Method
Demberg08	51,502	10	200,684	20,000	Eye-tracking
Mitchell10	5,370	10	53,704	5,300	Eye-tracking
McDonald03	2,262	23	31,242	1,350	Eye-tracking
Monsalve12	?	54	132,298	2,449	Self-paced reading
Boston08	1,138	222	167,499	754	Eye-tracking
Roark09	883	23	20,309	883	Self-paced reading

For similar study on French, there exists only one resource (the French part of the Dundee corpus (Kennedy et al., 2003)), but which is not publically available. This situation leads us to the project to build a new large resource for French, associating syntactic information, eye-tracking data and difficulty prediction. The pilot study presented hereafter has been realized in order to check the viability of the overall project.

3.1 Experimental design

One of our goal is to validate the experimental design. Our pilot study consisted in acquiring eye-movement data for 13 subjects reading an extract of the French Treebank (herefater *FTB*, (Abeillé et al., 2003)). The *FTB* is a set of articles from the newspaper *Le Monde*. Most of these articles are in the economical field, which does not fit well with the idea of natural reading. However, we selected from this corpus several extracts that seemed to us less technical in terms of semantic contents.

The eye-tracking device is a *Tobii 60 Hz* [3]. The selected subcorpus used in this experiment is made of 6 articles of variable length (from 3 to 6 minutes of reading time), each of them presented to the reader as a succession of slides. Participants have to press a key to access to the next slide. Once the key pressed, an empty frame with a target cursor indicating the position of the first line beginning the next slide is presented during three seconds, followed by the text slide. A calibration of the *Tobii* machine is proposed before reading each article and a three minutes pause between articles has been observed, filled by an informal discussion with the experimenter about the content of the article. The overall session last 45 minutes in average for each participant.

Each slide contains from 4 to 7 lines. Sentences were constrained to appear on a single slide, and the text is not right justified, tokens too long to enter the current line are printed on the

[3] In parallel, we will compare our data with their counterparts obtained using an Eye-link II system (these data are on the process to be acquired at LLF by B. Hemforth).

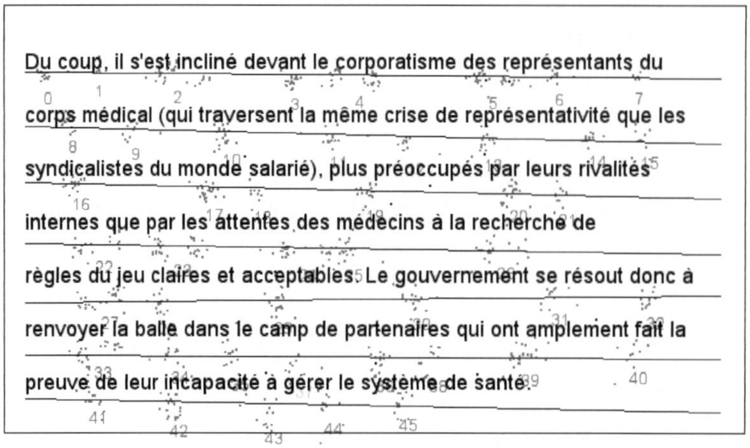

Figure 1: *An example of the slides presented. Red dots give the gaze positions recorded by the Tobii system at a 17 milliseconds rate. Horizontal lines represent the lines model fitted to the slide. The lines model allows to associate the gaze fixations (the clusters of points appearing on the figure) with the words of the text.*

next line. The text is printed on 800 × 600 pixels slides using an Arial font of size 18 with line spacing of size 26 pixels (an example is presented figure 1). The participant is positioned at a 60 cm distance of the screen, which implies a 30 pixels precision on *Tobii* measurements or equivalently a two characters horizontal precision and half line spacing in vertical precision.

The design of the experiment has been done thanks to a software we have developed (the generic designing software coming with *Tobii* being not suited for a full-text reading experiment). Our system automatically generates the slides and associates to each word its size in pixels as well as its precise spatial location. This renders straightforward the specification of each word (or set of words) as *"area-of-interest"* for the eye-tracking system. The overall corpus is made of 80 slides, 198 sentences split on 549 lines, which contains 6,572 tokens (5,696 words and 876 punctuation marks), which comes to 75,077 data points (a reasonable size in comparison with existing resources, see previous section).

3.2 Data post-processing

Our software also takes in charge data post-processing. In particular, one of the main problem consists in associating a sequence of eye movements with a line: the fact that backward movements (i.e. regressions) as well as line jumps are frequent renders difficult the association of a fixation aera with a word. We developed a specific algorithm to fit a line model to gaze measurements (see figure 1). The lines model allows to establish a geometrical relation between the set of fixations and the tokens of the slide. A parameter measures the quality of the fit. It is used to discard the slides for which the matching between fixations and tokens is problematic. For the present pilot experiment, the ratio of discarded slides reaches 12%. However, all the slides presented possess valid measurements for at least 9 participants over the group of 13 subjects.

Fixations are formed from individual gaze measurements by use of standard clustering techniques[4]. The minimal duration time has been fixed to 85 ms and a maximal clustering length of 30 pixels has been adopted (or a two characters length, which is the precision of the *Tobii* device). First and last fixations of the slide are trimmed if problematic (e.g. at the end of the reading, it is not rare that the reader's gaze wanders over the slide before pressing the next slide key). We therefore obtain the list of fixations and their associated parameters (position, starting time, ending time, ...). Thanks to the lines model (which gives the line the fixation belongs to) and the horizontal coordinate of the fixation, the closest token is associated with the fixation. Herein, we choose to associate fixation only to words, so by construction punctuation marks have zero reading time.

From the fixations list, we collect for each token of the slide and for each participant the oculomotor quantities of interest such as the first pass duration time, total reading time, number of fixations, and so on. This information is enriched for each token by metric and positioning information (length in pixels, number of characters, line index, position index in the line, ...) and later on in the analysis with linguistic information (morphosyntactic category, lexical frequency, ...). For the overall $6,572$ tokens of the corpus, we finally obtain $75,077$ oculomotor measurements for the set of 13 participants ($10,359$ over $85,436$ have been discarded due to lines model problem). Among them, $34,598$ have a null total duration time ($11,388$ correspond to punctuation marks, the $23,210$ remaining correspond to skipped words, i.e. words with no associated fixation). The ratio of skipped words (over the total number of words) is around 36% for our corpus of french newspaper articles.

The comparison of our pilot experiment with similar works (e.g. the french part of the Dundee corpus (Kennedy et al., 2003)) does not reveal significant difference concerning the global reading parameters such the mean fixation duration, saccade ratio, regression ratio, ... It means that the experimental setup chosen (e.g. large font size, spacious layout, ...), even if far from ecological reading condition, does not pertube the participant reading task. Similarly, the low sampling rate (one measurement each 17 milliseconds) and the relatively poor spatial precision of the Tobii device does not affect the average values of the global reading parameters. An accurate comparison of the Tobii and Eye-link II results will be conducted as soon as the Eye-link II data will be available for our reading material.

4 Analysis

The analysis relies on the paradigm that the reading times are a tracer of the linguistic complexity. In the present pilot study, our main objective restricts to study what can we learn about linguistic difficulty from reading time measurements. In particular, to model the reading strategy (e.g. when and where fixations occur) is out of the scope of the analysis. Therefore, the model we propose does not contain low-level variables describing reading strategy except the word length which accounts for the time spent to decode the characters of the words.

Motivations leading us to choose this strategy are twofold. First, we desire to draw robust conclusions concerning the linguistic difficulty, independent of a peculiar choice for the model describing the reading strategy. Second, as far as possible, we will try to limit the number of variables entering the statistical model. Indeed, the difficulty to interpret the resulting fitted values of a linear model (mixed or not) increases with the number of dimensions (i.e. the number of variables), especially when all these variables are strongly statistically dependent.

[4]A complete presentation of the algorithms implemented herein as well as a comparison with the state-of-the-art (see (Holmqvist et al., 2011)) will be proposed in a forthcoming paper.

In that case, the parameters space becomes highly instable, and the addition (or removal) of one variable in the model may dramatically change the resulting fitted coefficients. This effect has to be avoided since the final interpretation eventually relies on the values of these fitted coefficients.

In the following subsection, we introduce the basic ingredients of the model. The multivariate regression analysis is performed subsection 4.2 where the main results are discussed.

4.1 The variables of the model

4.1.1 Reading time

In the present study, we will focus on the total reading time measurement, defined as the sum of duration lengths for all the fixations on the area spanned by the token, including backward fixations.

In order to compare the token reading times measured for the different participants, we will first proceed to a normalization. Each participant P possess its own reading velocity $V(P)$ which can be estimated on the corpus. For each participant, the sum over the slides not discarded of the tokens total reading time $D(P)$ and tokens length $L(P)$ (for example the length in pixels) are computed. The mean reading velocity of the participant is then given by $V(P) = L(P)/D(P)$. By introducing the average reading velocity over the participants $\overline{V}$, we can form the normalized total reading time for token t and participant P :

$$D(t,P) = \frac{V(P)}{\overline{V}} \times \texttt{total reading time}(t,P) \tag{1}$$

Note that this transformation affects also the minimal threshold of 85 milliseconds (i.e. the minimal duration for a fixation).

Since participants were asked to read the same texts, it could be interesting to introduce the notion of *average reader*. The token reading time of the average reader $\overline{D}(t)$ is defined as the average of the normalized reading times over the participants (when this measurement is available) :

$$\overline{D}(t) = \sum_{P} D(t,P) \Big/ \sum_{P} 1 \tag{2}$$

It has been observed (Lorch and Myers, 1990) that averaging over participants is source of information loss for the low-level variables describing reading strategy (e.g. landing position, launch distance, ...). However, we are herein not concerned by this potential problem since low-level variables are not included in our model.

4.1.2 Word length

Reading times are known to depend on the word lengths (see (Rayner, 1998) for a review of the literature). For a token t, we choose to include this metric information by considering the number of characters of the token :

$$L(t) = \texttt{number of characters}(t) \tag{3}$$

The $L(t)$ variable accounts for the time spent to decode the characters of the token. Other metric information (landing position, previous word fixated, ...) is herein not considered.

4.1.3 Lexical information

The frequency of the word is another variable of our model. Frequent words are red faster, which can be interpreted either as a lexical access facility or as a predictability effect. The variable used herein is minus the logarithm of the lexical probability of the token form :

$$F(t) = -\log P(\mathtt{form(t)}) \tag{4}$$

This quantity is computed from the frequencies obtained in the LPL French lexicon augmented by the words of the *French Treebank*. Tokens not in the lexicon (punctuation marks, numbers, ...) have received a special treatment.

4.1.4 Morphosyntactic surprisal

The classical surprisal model being very sensitive to the parser performance, we use a new measure relying on morphosyntactic analysis (Blache and Rauzy, 2011). The idea consists in making the same kind of differential measure as for surprisal (Hale, 2001), but using POS-tagging instead of parsing.

POS-tagging builds during the process a set of solutions for the sequence of tokens. Each solution corresponds to an alternative when associating the set of morphosyntactic categories (tags) to the lexical form of the token (POS). Let's call $Sol_i(t)$ the ith solution at position t,

$$Sol_i(t) = c_{1,i} \ldots c_{t,i} \tag{5}$$

where $c_{t,i}$ is the morphosyntactic category associated to the token at position t for solution $Sol_i(t)$. The probability of the solution $Sol_i(t)$ is obtained recursively by Bayes formulae :

$$P(Sol_i(t)) = P(c_{t,i}|Sol_i(t-1)) \times P(Sol_i(t-1)) \tag{6}$$

where $P(Sol_i(t-1))$ is the probability of the solution i at position $t-1$ and $P(c_{t,i}|Sol_i(t-1))$ is the conditional probability of category $c_{t,i}$ given the left context $Sol_i(t-1) = c_{1,i} \ldots c_{t-1,i}$. The relative contribution of each solution can be obtained thanks to the introduction of the density function $\rho_i(t)$:

$$\rho_i(t) = \frac{P(Sol_i(t))}{A(t)}, \ \mathtt{with}\ A(t) = \sum_i P(Sol_i(t)) \tag{7}$$

Following (Hale, 2001), the morphosyntactic surprisal at position t for each solution $Sol_i(t)$ is :

$$S_i(t) = -\log \frac{P(Sol_i(t))}{P(Sol_i(t-1))} = -\log P(c_{t,i}|c_{1,i} \ldots c_{t-1,i}) \tag{8}$$

and the overall surprisal is :

$$S(t) = \sum_i \rho_i(t) S_i(t) \tag{9}$$

The morphosyntactic surprisal is an *unlexicalized* surprisal (see (Demberg and Keller, 2008)) in the sense that it does not capture the lexical probability of the form (that information is however included in the model section 4.1.3). The morphosyntactic surprisal accounts for two distinct types of difficulty: one related to the predictability of the proposed tag in context (high predictibility leads to low surprisal), the other coming from the effective number of solutions maintained in parallel due lexical form ambiguity (the higher is this effective number, the higher is the surprisal).

Without entering into details (a complete presentation can be found in (Blache and Rauzy, 2011)), the contextual probabilities entering equations 6 and 8 are learned on the *GraceLPL* French corpus augmented by the *French Treebank*. Adding the corpus under treatment allows to avoid infinite value for surprisal (e.g. the cases present in the corpus to tag but no met in the training corpus).

4.2 Model and results

The aim is herein to quantify the relative effects of the variables mentioned above on reading time measurements. At first approximation, a simple linear model is assumed :

$$D = \alpha_L \, L + \alpha_F \, F + \alpha_S \, S + D_0 + \epsilon \tag{10}$$

where the slopes α_L, α_F and α_S measure the strength of the effect of the explanatory variables L, F and S respectively, D_0 is the intercept of the model and the residuals ϵ account for what remains unexplained by the model.

4.2.1 Analysis at the token scale

We applied a multivariate linear regression to the $75,077$ individual normalized reading time measurements. For convenience, the explanatory variables have been previously scaled (zero mean and unit variance), in such way that the slope gives directly the strength of the effect on the duration time. All the slopes are found positive (which was expected) and highly significant. However, a closer analysis reveals that the residuals of the model are strongly dependent on the predicted values (see figure 2).

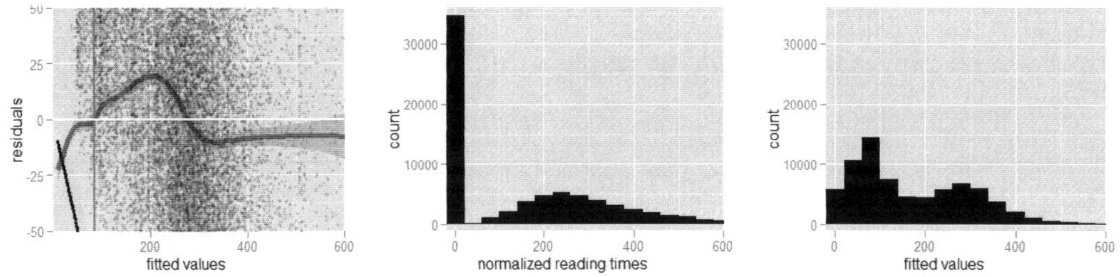

Figure 2: *For individual reading time measurements, the residuals of the linear model fit are plotted versus the fitted values. For a valid fit, the moving average of residuals (blue curve) is expected to match the x-axis within its error bars. The minimal fixation duration is represented by the vertical red line. The histogram of the normalized reading times and of the fitted values are also shown.*

The inspection of the normalized reading times and predicted values histograms of figure 2 explains why the linear model fails to fit reading time measurements. About 46% of the tokens have null reading time (67% of them are skipped words, the remaining 33% consists in punctuation marks which have null reading time by construction). The explanatory variables entering the right term of equation 10 does not present such discrete bimodal distribution.

There is therefore little hope that a linear combination of these variables can successfully describe the data.

In order to minimize the problem of null reading times, two modifications are brought to the model. First, a binary parameter N_{pm} which specify whether the token is a punctuation mark or not is added to the linear model, i.e.

$$D = \alpha_L L + \alpha_F F + \alpha_S S + \alpha_{pm} N_{pm} + D_0 + \epsilon \tag{11}$$

The second modification concerns the reading times to fit. Because of the average over the participants, the average reading times introduced section 4.1.1 is less susceptible to present a bimodal distribution. The multivariate regression is thus applied on the 6,572 average reading times of the corpus including the binary parameter to deal with punctuation marks. The results are presented figure 3. The modified linear model is unable to describe the average reading times distribution. As expected, the distribution of the average reading times does not present the bimodal trend of the individual reading times histogram. However, the same dependency is found between the predicted values and residuals of the fit: short predicted reading times are predicted not enough short and long ones not enough long. This observation suggests that skipped words are not just skipped because they are frequent and short (in that case, the model will have explained the effect) and that this skipping word strategy is shared by the group of participants. The linear model misses an ingredient to account for this effect.

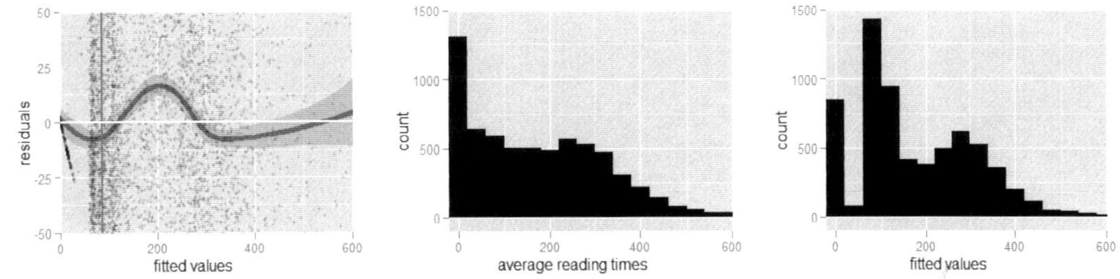

Figure 3: *Same plots as figure 2 for the average reading times over the participants.*

The problem is mainly due the presence of null reading time measurements in the data. One solution could be to remove them from the analysis. However statistics on truncated data, even if feasible in theory (see for example (Breen, 1996)), are often a tricky business in practice. Because a part of the genuine distribution has been removed, standard statistical recipes do not apply securely and the estimators of the model parameters are found biased in general. While some techniques exist to correct on these bias, they may require a full knowledge of the explanatory variables distributions and their dependencies, which is difficult to achieve in practice. We will not pursue this way.

A second solution could be to make use of a reading model which account for the skipped word phenomena. However again, our original aim was to make use of reading time measurements to learn about the syntactic complexity. As far as it is possible, we would like that our conclusions remain independent of a particular choice concerning the reading model used. We propose next subsection an alternative solution.

4.2.2 Analysis at larger scale

Our alternative solution is based on the following remark. All the variables entering the linear model are *extensive variables*[5], which means that they are globally additive under scale change. For example, the total duration time for a group of N tokens is the sum of the individual total reading time of the N tokens. Similarly, the property holds for the tokens length, the tokens frequency and as mentioned by (Smith and Levy, 2008), for the surprisal measure. Therefore, nothing prevents us to change the scale of the analysis, by considering group of adjacent tokens rather than working at the token scale.

We experimented this approach by forming groups of consecutive tokens (with the additional constraint that the tokens belong to the same line). The mutivariate regressions were performed on the summed quantities (summed average reading times, summed lengths, ...). The dependency between the predicted values of the fit and the residuals decreases as the size of the group increases. The fit becomes acceptable above the scale of 5 tokens. At this scale, it seems that the erroneous predicted reading times compensate each others (i.e. short versus long reading times) and provide us with a valid prediction for the reading time of the group as a whole.

This observation leads us to search for a natural scale grounded on linguistic information. Figure 4 displays for each morphosyntactic categories the boxplot of the number of participants having fixated the tokens. We remark that two populations emerges: the content words (adjectives, adverbs, nouns and verbs) with a high fixated count and the function words (determiners, auxiliaries, prepositions, ...) with a low fixated count.

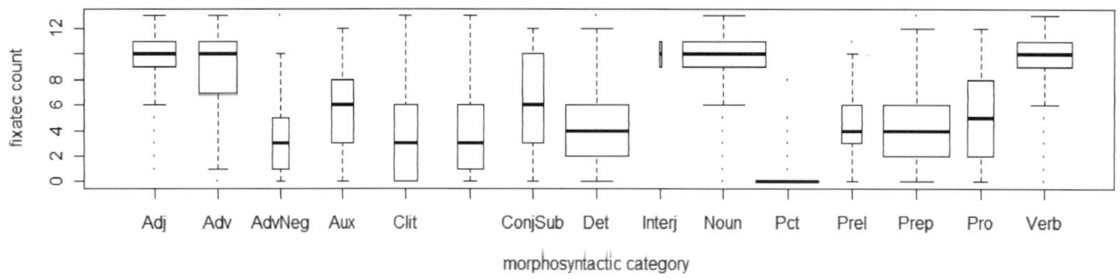

Figure 4: *Boxplot of the number of participants having fixated the tokens in function of the morphosyntactic category of the tokens.*

In the field of syntax, there exists a unit which groups the function words with their associated content word: the *chunk* (Abney, 1991). It remains to check whether the chunk scale is a good candidate for our analysis. Because chunks have variable sizes, we added to the linear model the variable N which represents the number of tokens in the chunk. The equation becomes :

$$D = \alpha_L L + \alpha_F F + \alpha_S S + \alpha_{pm} N_{pm} + \alpha_N N + D_0 + \epsilon \qquad (12)$$

Our corpus contains 2,842 chunks, the average number of tokens by chunk is 2.31. The results of the multivariate regression fit are shown figure 5. A slight dependency of the residuals is still

[5]The notion of *extensive* versus *intensive* variables comes from Thermodynamics and Statistical Physics.

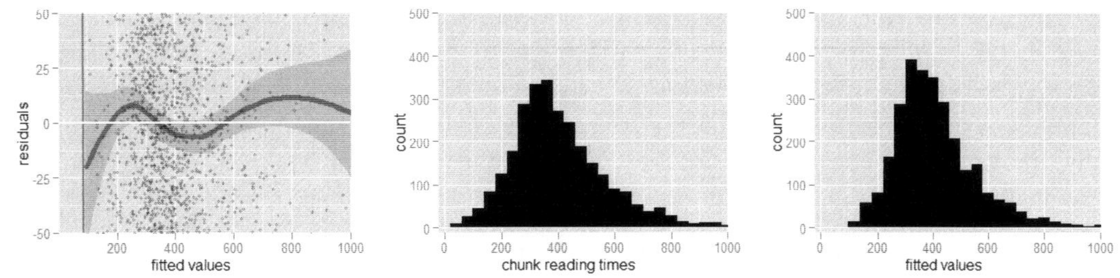

Figure 5: *Same plots as figure 2 for average reading times at the chunk scale. The grey envelope represents 1-σ error bars on the moving average.*

Variable	Estimate	Std. Error	Pr(>|t|)
(Intercept)	422.775	2.307	<2e-16 ***
L_{scaled}	89.388	2.798	<2e-16 ***
F_{scaled}	91.527	4.429	<2e-16 ***
S_{scaled}	22.345	2.696	<2e-16 ***
N_{scaled}	-35.382	4.618	2.51e-14 ***
$N_{punctuation}$	-37.156	4.248	<2e-16 ***

Table 1: The slopes, standard errors and statistical significance for the variables entering the linear fit.

present (the maximal amplitude is about 7 milliseconds on residuals), but its effect has been considerably lessening if compared with the analysis at the token scale (see figure 3).

Table 1 summarizes the amplitudes of the effect for each variable of the linear model. The residuals standard error is of 101 ms and the multiple R-squared of 0.687. In average, a chunk is red in 422 ms. The influence of the chunk length and the chunk frequency are of the same order (around 90 ms, or 20% of the average reading time). The contribution of morphosyntactic surprisal is slighter, 22 ms or 5% of the signal. A negative effect is found for the number of tokens. At equal values for length, frequency and morphosyntactic surprisal, chunks containing more tokens are red slower. Note that the amplitudes of all these effects are considerably larger than the 7 ms maximal dependency bias remaining in the fit. We can thus conclude securely that these effects are real.

5 Results and perspectives

The first goal of this work was to develop and evaluate a difficulty model based on *morpho-syntactic surprisal*. The results obtained with eye-tracking data show that our model is a good reading time predictor. This result is interesting for several reasons. First, it replicates for French similar results obtained for other languages. Second, it shows that morpho-syntactic surprisal is a good predicting variable. Because this difficulty measure is very robust and independent from any syntactic formalism, it is possible to use for any linguistic material, including spoken language: this opens the way to future experiments on predicting difficulty in natural interaction.

Evaluating this model led us to other interesting theoretical, methodological and technical results. In particular, we have shown that it is possible to keep all original data, including null reading time tokens. Variables of the linear model being additive under scale change, it becomes possible to take into consideration set of tokens as fixation area. Interestingly, considering syntactic chunks as fixation area provides very good result (reducing in a considerable extent the dependency of the residuals). This observation allows to avoid the important data reduction usually applied by other works. Moreover, it gives an experimental support to the idea that reading is done at he level of chunks instead of words.

More generally, these results has to be situated in the perspective of the development of a generic difficulty model that would integrate (1) parameters from different linguistic domains and (2) high level effects such as *cumulativity* (Keller, 2005) or *compensation* (Blache, 2011), increasing or decreasing difficulty. Our objective with such a generic model is to answer at three questions: where, how and why difficulties occur. This long-term goal is based on the idea that the basic elements of the integration process are variable in granularity: this process can indeed relies on words, but also on larger units such as phrases, prosodic units or discursive segments.

Last, but not least, this study led to the construction of a high-level linguistic resource: a treebank enriched with eye-tracking data plus difficulty measures. Such resource will be of great interest in the perspective of the new field of experimental syntax.

Acknowledgments

Vera Demberg, Stéphanie Ducrot, Sophie Dufour and John Hale are cheerfully thanked for fruitful discussions.

References

Abeillé, A., Clément, L., and Toussenel, F. (2003). Building a treebank for french. In Abeillé, A., editor, *Treebanks*, Kluwer, Dordrecht.

Abney, S. (1991). Parsing by chunks. In *Principle-Based Parsing. Kluwer Academic Publishers*, pages 257–278.

Blache, P. (2011). Evaluating language complexity in context: New parameters for a constraint-based model. In *CSLP-11, Workshop on Constraint Solving and Language Processing*.

Blache, P. and Rauzy, S. (2011). Predicting linguistic difficulty by means of a morpho-syntactic probabilistic model. In *Proceedings of PACLIC 2011, december 2011*, Singapour.

Boston, M. F., Hale, J., Kliegl, R., Patil, U., and Vasishth, S. (2008). Parsing costs as predictors of reading difficulty: An evaluation using the potsdam sentence corpus. *Journal of Eye Movement Research*, 2(1):1–12.

Breen, R. (1996). *Regression models : Censored, Sample selected or Truncated Data*. Sage Publications Ltd.

Demberg, V. and Keller, F. (2008). Data from eye-tracking corpora as evidence for theories of syntactic processing complexity. In *Cognition*, volume 109, Issue 2, pages 193–210.

Gibson, E. (1998). Linguistic complexity: locality of syntactic dependencies. *Cognition*, 68:1–76.

Gibson, E. (2000). The dependency locality theory: A distance-based theory of linguistic complexity. In *Image*. A. Marantz, Y. Miyashita, W. O'Neil (Edts).

Hale, J. (2001). A probabilistic earley parser as a psycholinguistic model. In *Proceeding of 2nd Conference of the North American Chapter of the Association for Computational Linguistics*, Pittsburgh, PA.

Hawkins, J. (2001). Why are categories adjacent. *Journal of Linguistics*, 37.

Holmqvist, K., Nystrom, M., Anderson, R., Dewhurst, R., Jaradzka, H., and van de Weijer, J. (2011). *Eye Tracking: A comprehensive guide to methods and measures*. Oxford Press.

Keller, F. (2005). Linear Optimality Theory as a Model of Gradience in Grammar. In *Gradience in Grammar: Generative Perspectives*. Oxford University Press.

Kennedy, A., Hill, R., and Pynte, J. (2003). The dundee corpus. In *Proceedings of the 12th European Conference on Eye Movements*.

Lorch, R. F. and Myers, J. L. (1990). Regression analyses of repeated measures data in cognitive research. *Journal of Experimental Psychology: Learning, Memory, and Cognition*, 16(1):149–157.

McDonald, S. A. and Shillcock, R. C. (2003). Low-level predictive inference in read- ing: The influence of transitional probabilities on eye movements. *Vision Research*, 43.

Mitchell, J., Lapata, M., Demberg, V., and Keller, F. (2010). Syntactic and semantic factors in processing difficulty: An integrated measure. *Proceedings of the 48th Annual Meeting of the Association for Computational Linguistics*, pages 196–206.

Monsalve, I. F., Frank, S. L., and Vigliocco, G. (2012). Lexical surprisal as a general predictor of reading time. In *Proceeding of EACL*.

Pynte, J., New, B., and Kennedy, A. (2009). On-line contextual influences during reading normal text: The role of nouns, verbs and adjectives. *Vision Research*, 49(5):544–552.

Rayner, K. (1998). Eye movements in reading and information processing: 20 years of research. *Psychological Bulletin*, 124:372–422.

Smith, N. J. and Levy, R. (2008). Optimal processing times in reading: a formal model and empirical investigation. In *Proceedings of the 30th Annual Meeting of the Cognitive Science Society*, pages 595–600.

Vasishth, S. (2003). Quantifying processing difficulty in human sentence parsing: The role of decay, activation, and similarity-based interference. In *Proceedings of the European Cognitive Science Conference 2003*.

Scanpaths in reading are informative about sentence processing

Titus von der Malsburg[1] *Shravan Vasishth*[1] *Reinhold Kliegl*[2]
(1) Department of Linguistics, University of Potsdam
(2) Department of Psychology, University of Potsdam
{malsburg vasishth kliegl}@uni-potsdam.de

ABSTRACT
Scanpaths, sequences of fixations of the eyes, have historically played an important role in eyetracking research but their use has remained highly limited until recently. Here, we summarize earlier research and argue that scanpaths are a valuable source of information for reading research, specifically in the study of sentence comprehension. We also discuss a freely available, open source scanpath analysis method that we used to evaluate theoretical claims about human parsing and about how the parser guides the eyes during reading. This scanpath analysis is shown to yield new information that was missed when traditional approaches were used to study theories about eye guidance during garden-pathing. We also show how relatively subtle scanpath effects can be detected when we report the scanpath analysis of a large eyetracking corpus. In sum, we argue that scanpath analyses are likely to serve as an increasingly important tool in reading research, and perhaps also in other areas where eyetracking is used, e.g., in studies using the visual world paradigm.

KEYWORDS: scanpaths, reading, eye movements, parsing.

---

1 Introduction

Over the last decades, eyetracking has been established as one of the most important tools for studying human language processing. Eyetracking studies contributed to the investigation of the lexical retrieval of words and the processing of syntax, semantics, and discourse. The two dominant experimental paradigms that have been used are reading studies and visual world studies. In reading studies, the movements of the eyes are recorded as sentences are read. Typical dependent variables are word-based duration measures such as the time the eyes dwell on a word before proceeding to the next word or the probability to move backwards from a word (regression probability). Increased dwell times and rates of regressions on a particular word are commonly interpreted as reflecting difficulty to process that word or one of the previous words (Rayner, 1998; Clifton et al., 2007; Vasishth et al., 2012). In visual word experiments, participants hear recordings of sentences while watching visual scenes. Typically, a scene is displayed in which one object is a target that is mentioned in the sentence; other objects serve as distractors. The amount of looks to the target object and their timing can uncover when various types of information come into play during comprehension (Huettig et al., 2011). For instance, if the target word is a pronoun ("him" vs "her"), the speed at which people converge with their gaze to the visual representation of the antecedent of the pronoun and the proportion of looks to distractors can be informative about the mechanisms underlying reference resolution (e.g., Kaiser et al., 2009).

Common to all these approaches is the fact that they considerably reduce the recorded information about eye movements. In reading studies, a word or small region is singled out for which a duration measure or a regression probability is computed, that is, the measure is aggregated across trials and participants. Eye movements that occurred before the eyes entered this region and after they left it are discarded. This approach is entirely reasonable if the effect of the experimental manipulation is focused to a particular critical region and if the effect of the manipulation is expected to be largely the same in all participants. In many cases, these assumptions may be reasonable; in this paper, however, we argue that they can be problematic in certain important situations. The issue is not limited to reading studies; information may be similarly lost in analyses of data acquired in visual world experiments. Eye movements in this type of experiment are most often evaluated using the percentage of looks to a region in the visual stimulus (target or distractor) as a function of time. This involves aggregating the data of all trials in a condition and the individual fixation sequences are lost. If there were several qualitatively different fixation patterns, reflecting different cognitive processes, these would not be identifiable in the aggregate. The purpose of these simplifications of the eyetracking data is (i) to get rid of irrelevant variance which could mask the effects of interest and (ii) to extract a dependent measure that can be analyzed using standard statistical tools. Clearly, simplification of the data is a trade-off: the raw data is difficult to interpret but an over-simplified signal can be misleading.

In this paper, we will focus on eye movements in reading and show that some theoretically important eye movement phenomena are not captured by the traditional eyetracking measures. These measures can therefore be misleading in some circumstances. In recent work, we introduced a new method for analyzing eye movements that addresses some of the issues with traditional measures. We will explain which problem exactly this method aims to solve and how the method works. Next, we will discuss how we used this method in (i) a reading experiment and (ii) an analysis of a large-scale eyetracking corpus. Before we start to describe this new method, it is useful to have a closer look at the data we are dealing with.

1.1 Eye movements in reading: What do they look like?

In this paper, we discuss our analyses of two sets of eyetracking data (these analyses are reported in von der Malsburg and Vasishth, 2012; von der Malsburg et al., 2012). The first data set was collected in a reading experiment that investigated the processing of Spanish garden-path sentences (von der Malsburg and Vasishth, 2012). The 70 Spanish native speakers tested in this study came from a relatively homogeneous population and the experimental sentences all followed a particular syntactic construction (average number of words: 18.5). Because of a temporary attachment ambiguity of an adverbial clause these sentences were somewhat difficult to process, but they still constitute an easy type of garden-path sentence. The design of the study resembles that of typical reading studies in sentence processing research: the conditions were minimally different from each other, the sentences had comparable length, and the presentation of items (pseudo-randomly intermixed with fillers) was counterbalanced in the standard manner. The second data set is the Potsdam Sentence Corpus (henceforth, the PSC), a database of eye movements recorded from 230 participants reading a set of 144 sentences (Kliegl et al., 2004). The participants ranged from teenagers to pensioners and came from diverse socioeconomic backgrounds. The sentence material consisted of simple German sentences (ranging from 5 to 11 words, average: 7.9) that were designed to represent a large variety of syntactic constructions. Thus, the PSC can be regarded as a representative sample of how the general population reads common sentence types.

How would a machine direct its eyes when reading a sentence? One obvious strategy would be to scan the words from left to right one at a time, looking on each word until it is fully processed and to move to the next when finished. The spatial pattern of fixations generated by such a reader would not be interesting because it would always be the same regardless of the sentence being read: a monotonic movement in one direction. All information about the underlying processes would be conveyed by the temporal dynamics. While human readers use a similar reading strategy, the targets of their saccades are far from being as predictable as those of our hypothetical reading machine. In the PSC, for instance, 19% of the saccades skip the next word (skipped words are typically short and have high frequency), 17% of the saccades result in another fixation on the current word, and 14% of the saccades are directed at previous words. Hence, only 50% of the saccades target the next word in the sentence. This means that even when people read simple sentences that do not pose any larger difficulties, they deviate considerably from a monotonous left-to-right reading style. Several factors have been shown to causes these deviations from a straight eye movement trajectory. They include oculo-motor constraints, lexical processing, and higher-level language processing (Rayner, 1998; Bicknell and Levy, 2011).

Fig. 1 shows eye movements from the PSC that were recorded when participants read the sentence in (1). This sentence has long words (easy to target) and canonical word order (easy to process). Of all sentences in the PSC, this one elicited the most regular reading patterns. The scanpaths in fig. 1 can therefore be seen as marking the lower bound on irregularity in scanpaths. Although the participants read this sentence mostly from left to right, the plot shows that in almost all trials words were skipped and that in several trials material was revisited.

(1) *Wolfgangs Töchter studieren Literatur und Maschinenbau.*
Wolfgang's daughters study literature and engineering.

When a sentence contains words that are difficult to integrate into the syntactic or semantic

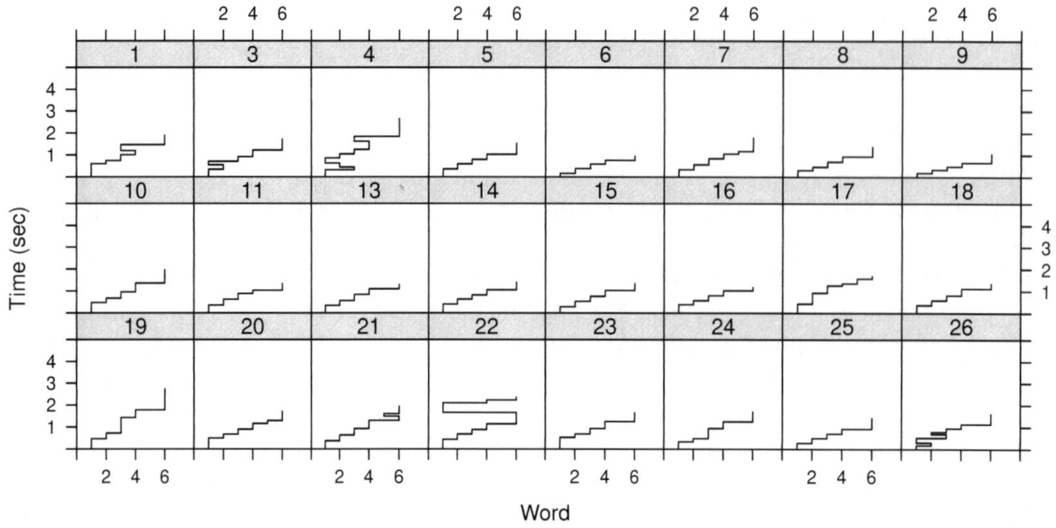

Figure 1: Eye movement as recorded in 24 trials in which participants read the sentence "Wolfgang's daughters study literature and engineering." Each panel shows how a specific participant read the sentence. Words are on the x-axis, time is on the y-axis, and the lines shows the trajectory of the eyes. In only three trials (7, 17, 20), the eyes proceeded strictly from word to word. In most trials the short word "and" was skipped. In several trials the eyes returned to earlier material (1, 3, 4, 21, 22, 26).

interpretation of the sentence, reading patterns can deviate even more from a straight unidirectional reading pattern. Quite early in psycholinguistic research, Frazier and Rayner (1982) demonstrated that encountering the disambiguating word in a garden-path sentence such as (2) can cause multi-fixation regressive eye movements which they interpreted as reflecting syntactic reanalysis. For instance, when reading the sentence in (2), readers have a tendency to interpret the noun phrase "the sock" initially as the object of "mending". However, when "fell" is encountered, it becomes clear that this role assignment cannot be maintained and the interpretation of the sentence has to be revised.

(2) While Mary was mending the sock fell off her lap.

At the time when Frazier and Rayner carried out their study, no statistical tools were available for analyzing the fixation patterns that ensued when the critical word was read. Therefore, they analyzed the data qualitatively. Later studies used quantitative measures to confirm that syntactic reanalysis causes complex regression patterns but the precise nature of these patterns could not be resolved (Meseguer et al., 2002; Mitchell et al., 2008). To illustrate what kind of data the authors of these studies were dealing with we selected 24 representative trials from an experiment that we conducted to investigate the same questions as those that Frazier and Rayner pursued (von der Malsburg and Vasishth, 2012). These trials are shown in fig. 2. In

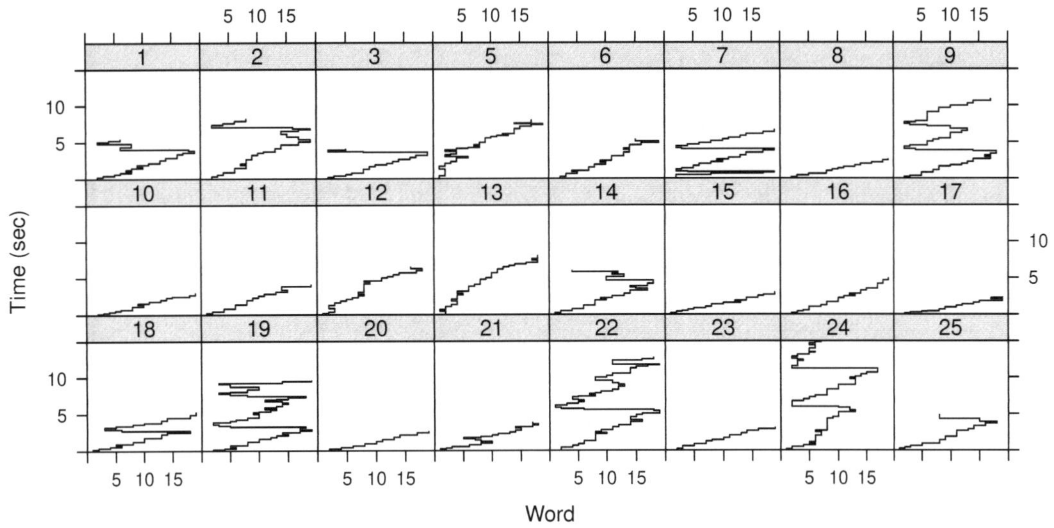

Figure 2: Eye movement as recorded in 24 trials in which participants read the sentences in (3) ("El profesor dijo ... "). Each panel shows how a specific participant read the sentence. Words are on the x-axis, time is on the y-axis, and the lines shows the trajectory of the eyes.

about 50% of the trials, the participants of this experiment produced regressive eye movements after they read the critical word in the sentence showing that sentence processing can have a dramatic impact on the gaze trajectory. In the vast majority of cases, these regressive eye movements consisted of several fixations, which rules out a trivial numerical representation of the gaze trajectory. The measures devised by earlier authors (Meseguer et al., 2002; Mitchell et al., 2008) reduced these fixation sequences (the scanpaths) to only the first backwards directed saccade following the fixation on the critical word. The benefit of this approach is that the distribution of landing sites of this saccade can be modeled using standard statistical tools; the drawback is that information about eye movement events following this first regressive saccade is lost. One goal of this paper is to show that this loss of information can have a critical impact on the inferences drawn from eye movement data.

Summarizing this section, we can say that, despite the linear nature of text, reading patterns are quite complex, and that they may contain important information about the cognitive processes underlying reading. The next section will describe a method that can be used to leverage that information.

2 Analyzing Scanpaths

The central problem when analyzing eye movement patterns (scanpaths) is that they are complex. A scanpath can consist of an arbitrary number of fixations and these fixations are described in three dimensions: two spatial dimensions (e.g. coordinates on the screen) and time (duration of a fixation). When we analyze traditional measures such as the first pass reading time of a word, we can compare all measurements by simply calculating their differences and we can calculate means, standard deviations, and confidence intervals to make inferences. In contrast to that it is unclear how two measurements should be compared if they consist of scanpaths. What is the mean of a set of scanpaths and how can we describe the variance? These questions could be answered if there was a vector representation of scanpaths in a common vector space but deriving such a representation is not trivial due to the variable length of scanpaths ranging from two fixations to an unbounded number of fixations. One way to derive a vector representation has been proposed by Josephson and Holmes (2002). The procedure is as following: calculate all pair-wise similarities of the scanpaths in a data set. Next, set up an n-dimensional vector space and for each scanpath randomly place a vector in this space. Then, use an iterative procedure that optimizes the positions of these vectors until their distances in the vector space approximate the previously calculated similarities of the corresponding scanpaths as well as possible (this procedure is called non-metric multidimensional scaling, Kruskal, 1964). These vector representations—we call them maps of scanpath space—have various desirable properties: scanpaths that are similar are located close to each other in the vector space and dissimilar scanpaths are far apart. This property allows us to apply clustering procedures to the map of scanpaths in order to identify categories of scanpath patterns. We can also calculate the variance in the scanpaths, identify an "average" scanpath (i.e., the scanpath in the center of gravity of a set), and locate the areas of highest density in order find scanpath patterns that occurred often.

The missing ingredient for these things to work is an appropriate similarity measure that captures the relevant properties of scanpaths. One proposal has been to use the Levenshtein distance (Brandt and Stark, 1997; Salvucci and Anderson, 2001) which quantifies the (dis)similarity of two sequences of symbols as the number of edit-operations that have to be performed on one sequence to transform it into the other (Levenshtein, 1966). These operations are deletion and insertion of a symbol and substitution of a symbol by another symbol. This measure can be applied to eye movements in the following way: partition the visual stimulus into regions and uniquely label each region with a letter. A sequence of fixations can then be represented by a sequence of letters in which the n-th letter specifies the location of the n-th fixation (see fig. 3 for an illustration).

The Levenshtein metric has many desirable properties such as the ability to deal with sequences of unequal length and being relatively cheap to compute.[1] However, it also has some important limitations. First, reading times are ignored completely because they are not part of the representation on which the Levenshtein metric operates (strings of letters). So whether a fixation in one scanpath that is not present in the other is long or short does not have any impact on the similarity score for these two scanpaths. The second limitation is that the similarity of two fixation sequences depends on how the visual stimulus was partitioned. If the regions are large, the scanpaths in a data set will on average be more similar to each other than when they are small because the probability that fixations coincide in the same region is higher if these regions are large. What is a reasonable partitioning? In reading, words serve reasonably well as regions of interest but there is no general answer to this question. The third limitation of the Levenshtein metric is that a deviation between two scanpaths in one fixation leads to an increase of the dissimilarity of 1 irrespective of whether the deviation is spatially large or small. That means that if a fixation in one scanpath is on a word and the corresponding fixation is not on the same word but really close, the two fixations will be counted as being as dissimilar as two

[1]The Needleman-Wunsch algorithm is commonly used to do the computation and takes processing time and memory resources proportional to the product of the lengths of the two sequences (Needleman and Wunsch, 1970).

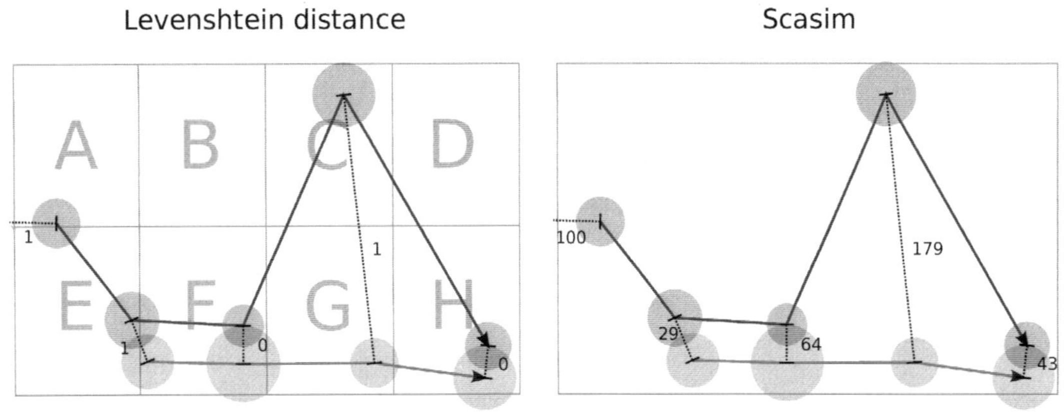

Figure 3: Two graphs illustrating how the Levenshtein metric and the Scasim measure calculate the similarity of two scanpaths. For the Levenshtein metric the stimulus has to be partitioned into regions (A, B, C, . . .) so that the scanpaths can be represented as symbol sequences. The blue scanpath is represented as AEFCH, the red one as FFGH. For every mismatch in these sequences the Levenshtein metric increases by one. The Scasim measure, on the other hand, does not require a partitioning of the stimulus. The coordinates and durations of the fixations are represented as continuous variables. The mismatch in the two scanpaths can then be quantified as a function of the spatial and temporal differences between the matching fixations. Differences in fixation durations (represented as the size of the circles) and spatial distances both contribute to the overall (dis)similarity of two scanpaths.

fixations that are really far apart. Research on oculo-motor control in reading has found that a word can be processed even if it is not in the center of the fovea (the high-resolution center of the visual field) but also when it is in the parafovea (Rayner, 1975). This means that a fixation close to a word can have similar consequences as a fixation *on* the word. Treating fixations close to a word as if they were far apart is therefore undesirable. In sum, the Levenshtein metric is a relatively crude measure for scanpath similarity because it deprives scanpaths of their temporal information and because it uses a very coarse-grained model of space. This situation prompted us to develop a new similarity measure for scanpaths, called Scasim, that is highly sensitive to the spatio-temporal properties of scanpaths (von der Malsburg and Vasishth, 2007, 2011).

2.1 The Scasim measure

Our measure uses the same general approach as the Levenshtein distance. The difference is the way we account for deviations in two scanpaths. Where the Levenshtein distance assigns a "cost" of 1 for every fixation that differs in two scanpaths, we assign a cost that is a function of the spatial locations and the fixation durations: if a fixation has to be deleted in one scanpath, the cost for that deletion is the duration of that fixation. Deleting a long fixation therefore leads to a larger overall dissimilarity between two scanpaths than deleting a short fixation. Similarly, the cost of inserting a fixation is simply the duration of the inserted fixation. The cost for substituting one fixation by another fixation depends on the durations and locations of the two fixations. If they have the same location, the cost of the substitution is simply the difference in their fixation durations. If the two fixations are extremely far apart, the cost is given by the sum of the fixation durations. There are two reasons for this choice. First, if the two fixations are long, this means that the spatial deviation between them is temporally longer and should therefore lead to increased overall dissimilarity. Second, this choice means that substituting two fixations that are extremely far apart amounts to the same dissimilarity as deleting one of the fixation and inserting the other. This property avoids discontinuities in the similarity function, e.g., when the duration of one fixation converges to zero. What is the dissimilarity when the two fixations are neither at the same location nor extremely far apart, i.e., if they are only somewhat spatially separated? In this case, the cost of the substitution is a weighted sum of the difference of the fixation durations and the sum of the fixation durations. The weights are a function of the spatial distance and are determined by a function that mimics the exponential drop in visual acuity of human vision (Daniel and Whitteridge, 1961; Rovamo et al., 1978).

Some useful properties of the resulting similarity measure that follow from these definitions are: (i) Partitioning of the stimulus in more or less arbitrary regions is not necessary because the measures is a continuous function of the coordinates and durations of the fixations in two scanpaths. (ii) The measure is theory-agnostic, i.e., it does not make any assumptions about the significance of certain types of eye movements, e.g., a regression in reading is not treated any different than any other eye movement pattern. (iii) Similarity scores can be efficiently computed with a variant of the Needleman-Wunsch algorithm (Needleman and Wunsch, 1970). See von der Malsburg and Vasishth (2011) for a detailed discussion of Scasim. See fig. 3 for an illustration showing how the similarity of two scanpaths is computed with Scasim.

There is not one true similarity measure for scanpaths and our measure constitutes only one possible way to quantify differences between scanpaths. What's similar and what's not really depends on the question being asked and while our measure may be useful in one type of analysis it may not be suitable in other types. Given that, it is not surprising that quite a few other similarity measures have recently been proposed which all have different properties and applications (Salvucci and Anderson, 2001; Cristino et al., 2010; Jarodzka et al., 2010; Mathôt et al., 2012; Coco and Keller, 2012). Unfortunately, there is no space here to describe these measures, but some are discussed and compared with Scasim in von der Malsburg and Vasishth (2011).

The next sections will describe two different ways in which we used the Scasim measure to analyze eye movements in reading.

3 Case study 1: Regression patterns during reanalysis

In von der Malsburg and Vasishth (2011, 2012) we investigated scanpaths in response to the disambiguation of Spanish garden-path sentences such as (3) (adapted from Meseguer et al., 2002).

(3) *El* *profesor* *dijo* *que* *los* *alumnos* *se levantaran* ...
The teacher said that the students had to stand up ...

a. [$_{AdvC}$ *cuando* *los* *directores* **entraron** *en la clase*].
[$_{AdvC}$ when the directors came into the classroom].

b. [$_{AdvC}$ *cuando* *los* *directores* **entraran** *en la clase*].
[$_{AdvC}$ when the directors come into the classroom].

c. $[_{AdvC}$	**si**	*los*	*directores*	*entraban*	*en la clase*].
$[_{AdvC}$	if	the	directors	come	into the classroom].

Sentences (3a) and (3b) contain an adverbial clause ("cuando los directores ...") which can initially be attached to the main verb of the sentence ("dijo") or to the embedded verb ("levantaran"). The correct attachment site is only determined when the verb of the adverbial phrase is read ("entraron" / "entraran") because the mood of this verb (indicative or subjunctive) agrees with either the main verb or the embedded verb. Low attachment to the embedded verb is preferred in Spanish in agreement with the late-closure principle (Frazier, 1979). Therefore the sentence processor experiences difficulty at "entraron" in (3a) because this word indicates that the initial attachment was incorrect. A revision of the attachment has to be carried out. In sentence (3c), the attachment is unambiguously clear at all times because the "si"-clause can only attach to "levantaran".

The main question that we investigated was: which strategy does the parser use to revise the interpretation of the sentence? Three hypotheses about the mechanisms underlying revision have been proposed in the literature (see Frazier & Rayner, 1982, for a detailed discussion). The *forward reanalysis hypothesis* states that reanalysis is carried out by means of normal parsing routines. The parser is assumed to return to the beginning of the sentence and to re-parse the sentence while looking for choice points at which the misanalysis can be prevented. The *backward reanalysis hypothesis* states that the parser switches to reverse gear, undoing parsing decisions word-by-word until the crucial choice point is reached (Kaplan, 1972). The *selective reanalysis hypothesis* posits that the parser intelligently identifies the problem and that it deploys targeted repair mechanisms (Frazier and Rayner, 1982). Under the additional assumption that the eyes are tightly coupled to the sentence processor (the eyes look at the word that is currently being processed; Just and Carpenter, 1980) these hypotheses afford clearly distinguishable predictions about scanpath patterns. According to forward reanalysis, the eyes should return to the beginning of the sentence and start a second pass over the material so far. According to backward reanalysis, the eyes should reverse the direction going backwards until the beginning of the ambiguous region is reached ("cuando") and should then switch back to normal forward operation. According to selective reanalysis, the eyes should perform targeted saccades to words that are affected by the reanalysis: the ambiguous region, the main, and the embedded verb.

To test for these patterns, we recorded eye movements from 70 participants who read sentences as in (3). Since no reanalysis is required in (3b) where the critical word ("entraran") only supports the preferred interpretation, any regressive scanpath patterns that occur more often in (3a) than in (3b) can be interpreted as reflecting reanalysis. Thus, one way to address the question about reanalysis strategies is to perform a cluster analysis of scanpath patters with the goal to identify qualitatively different types of scanpaths and to see if one or several of these types occur more often in condition (3a) than in (3b).

3.1 Analysis

The complete analysis was carried out in GNU-R (R Development Core Team, 2009). We first extracted from all trials regressive scanpaths that occurred after the critical word was read. Next, we used our Scasim measure to calculate the pair-wise similarities of all these regression patterns. This can be done with a function called `Scasim` which is freely available from the authors.[2] This function takes a data frame (basically a table) as input which contains,

[2] `http://www.ling.uni-potsdam.de/~malsburg`

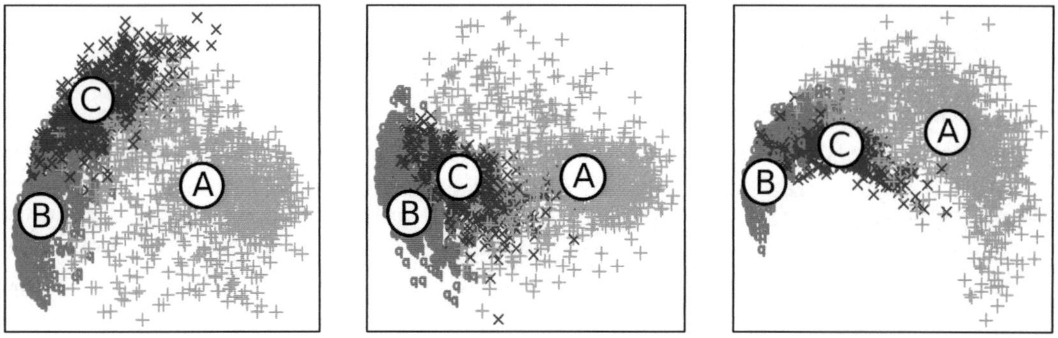

Figure 4: Three projections of the 7-dimensional map of scanpaths calculated for the analysis of scanpaths recorded in our Spanish experiment. Each point is a scanpath. The colors indicate membership to the three clusters (A, B, C) that were identified in the cluster analysis.

chronologically ordered, a line for every fixation in the data set. One column identifies the trial to which a fixation belongs, other columns specify the x and y coordinates and the duration of a fixation. The resulting matrix of similarity scores was then used to fit a map of scanpath space, i.e., a n-dimensional vector space with a vector for each regressive scanpath (see fig. 4). This was done using the function `isoMDS` from the package `MASS` which performs multidimensional scaling. Once the vector representation of scanpaths is available, a large range of statistical methods can be used to analyze the variance in scanpaths. We chose mixture of Gaussian modeling for the cluster analysis. Mixture models describe the distribution of data points using a set of multivariate Gaussians each of which represents one cluster. One important benefit over other clustering procedures, such as k-means, is that mixture models can identify overlapping clusters based on their distributional properties. The parameters of the Gaussians (position, spread, orientation) were calculated using expectation maximization (package `mclust`, Fraley and Raftery, 2002, 2007). A Bayesian information criterion was used to determine the optimal number of clusters (Schwarz, 1978).

The cluster analysis identified three broad classes of scanpath patterns which can be seen in the map of scanpaths in fig. 4. What scanpath pattern do these classes represent? A distribution of reaction times can be characterized by calculating its mean. Similarly we can characterize a cluster by identifying its center of gravity (the mean of the multivariate Gaussian). The scanpaths that are closest to that center can be seen as being prototypical for that cluster. Fig. 5 shows one prototypical scanpath for each of the three clusters that we found. In one pattern (A), the eyes reread the sentence as predicted by the forward reanalysis hypothesis. In another pattern (B), the eyes returned from the disambiguating region ("entraron/entraran") to the ambiguous region. In the third pattern (C), the eyes returned from the spill-over region ("en la clase") to the disambiguating region.

Pattern A (rereading) occurred more often in sentences as in (3a) in which the preferred interpretation is invalidated, suggesting that rereading reflects a reanalysis strategy. It was also found that readers with high working memory capacity produced this pattern more often than readers with a low working memory score. In the context of other results obtained in

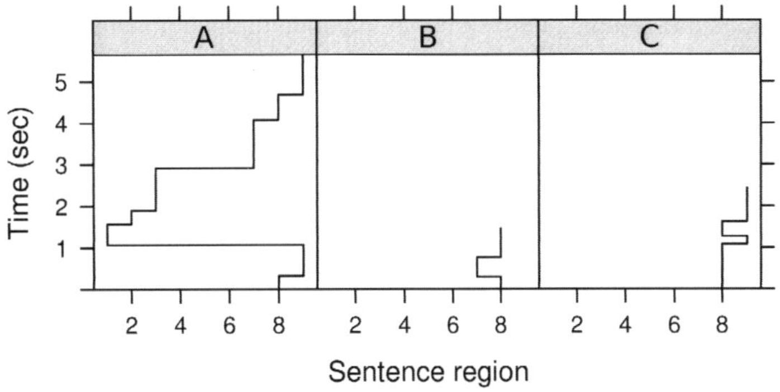

Figure 5: Prototypical scanpaths for three clusters identified in the cluster analysis of the scanpaths recorded in our Spanish study. These scanpaths were located at the center of gravity of the three clusters shown in fig. 4. In A, the eyes returned to the beginning of the sentences after having read the disambiguating word in region 8 and then reread the sentence. In B, the eyes rapidly regressed from the disambiguating word to the ambiguous region 7. In C, the eyes returned from the spill-over region 9 to the disambiguating region.

that study, this was interpreted as showing that high-capacity readers commit more eagerly to an attachment decision—and consequently have to revise these decisions more often—than low-capacity readers who were hypothesized to leave the attachment occasionally unspecified in order to preserve resources. Pattern C (revisiting the disambiguating word) occurred equally often in the temporarily ambiguous conditions (3a,b) but less often in the unambiguous condition (3c). The difference between sentences in conditions (3a) and (3b) was only one letter ("entraron" vs. "entraran") and it seems likely that type C regressions served to increase the certainty about what has been read in cases were the targeted word was decisive for the attachment of the adverbial clause (c.f. Bicknell and Levy, 2010). See von der Malsburg and Vasishth (2012) for more details.

Various aspects of these results suggest that analyses of scanpath patterns can contribute substantially to the interpretation of eyetracking data. We will briefly discuss two ways in which an analysis of traditional eyetracking measures would have missed important information in the eyetracking record.

First, Meseguer et al. (2002) found a high rate of regressions from the postdisambiguation region to regions close to the beginning of the sentence in an experiment that used almost the same sentences as ours. Their study also found that these regressions occurred more often in the garden-path condition. Meseguer and colleagues suspected that these regressions were targeted at the main verb of the sentence ("dijo") which was the true attachment site in these sentences and therefore argued in support of selective reanalysis which predicts these eye movements. However, examining scanpaths in cluster A (rereading), shows that regions close to the beginning of the sentence were often used as a stepping-stone on the way to the first word. This suggests that the main verb may not have been the actual target of regression triggered by disambiguation; rather, saccades to the main verb may have been the result of an undershoot on the way to the first word where rereading was initiated. This shows that the functional interpretation of saccades analysed in isolation can be problematic and it shows that scanpath analyses can help to avoid misinterpretations.

Second, working memory was found to modulate the rate of pattern A scanpaths (rereading) and pattern B scanpaths (regressions to the disambiguating region). However, the effects were different for these two types of scanpaths. There was no effect of working memory on the rate of pattern C scanpaths (revisiting the disambiguating region). A traditional regression measure such as regression probability conflates these effects by aggregating across the three functionally different types of scanpaths. The resulting pattern of effects is difficult to interpret. Indeed, if only regression probability were to be analyzed in the above case, qualitatively different effects of working memory on scanpaths may cancel each other out so that no influence of working memory would be detected at all. This shows that separating qualitatively different eye movement phenomena can in some situations reveal effects that would otherwise go unnoticed.

4 Case study 2: Scanpath variance in general reading

Our scanpath analysis of regressions in response to garden-pathing has shed new light on the mechanisms underlying the processing of ambiguous material. Can scanpaths also be informative about other processes involved in reading? One way to answer this question empirically is to analyze a database containing eye movements for a variety of constructions (e.g., the Potsdam Sentence Corpus, PSC) and to investigate the factors that influence scanpaths. These factors may include oculo-motor, sentence processing constraints, and individual difference in readers. In von der Malsburg et al. (2012), we reviewed the literature and identified three variables that should influence scanpath patterns. The effects of these variables have previously only been shown using simplifying, word-based eyetracking measures such as regression probability. The first variable is the syntactic processing difficulty of a sentence. In a wide range of studies, it has been found that if a word is difficult to integrate with the sentence fragment read so far, the result is often an increased rate of regressive eye movements (see Clifton et al., 2007, for a review). The second variable influencing scanpaths is the length of words. The literature on oculo-motor control in reading has found that short words are skipped more often (Brysbaert and Vitu, 1998; Kliegl et al., 2004; Drieghe et al., 2005) and that the eyes often return to skipped words (Vitu and McConkie, 2000; Engbert et al., 2005). The third variable is the age of readers: older readers skip words more often and also regress more often than young readers (Kliegl et al., 2004; Rayner et al., 2006). The effects of all three variables have also been documented for the PSC (Kliegl et al., 2004; Boston et al., 2008).

The goals of our scanpath analysis of the PSC were two-fold: First, we wanted to validate our scanpath measure. If the measure does what it is supposed to do, it should recover the scanpath effects that the literature hinted at. Analyzing the PSC can be seen as a particularly hard test because, as we reported above, the sentences were easy and the eyes went relatively straightforwardly from left to right; in other words, the scanpath effects in the PSC are presumably relatively subtle. The second goal of this study was to model, for the first time, the joint effects of the three variables, which had been studied in separate research fields (research on sentence processing, oculo-motor control, and cognitive aging), and their interactions.

In contrast to the scanpath analysis of syntactic reanalysis, we were not interested in identifying categories of scanpaths but in the degree to which the eyes deviate from a regular reading pattern. This irregularity of the scanpath can be quantified on the basis of maps of scanpaths similar to those described above. We used a similar procedure to calculate 144 of these maps, one for each of the 144 sentences in the PSC. Each of the 230 points on a map represents how

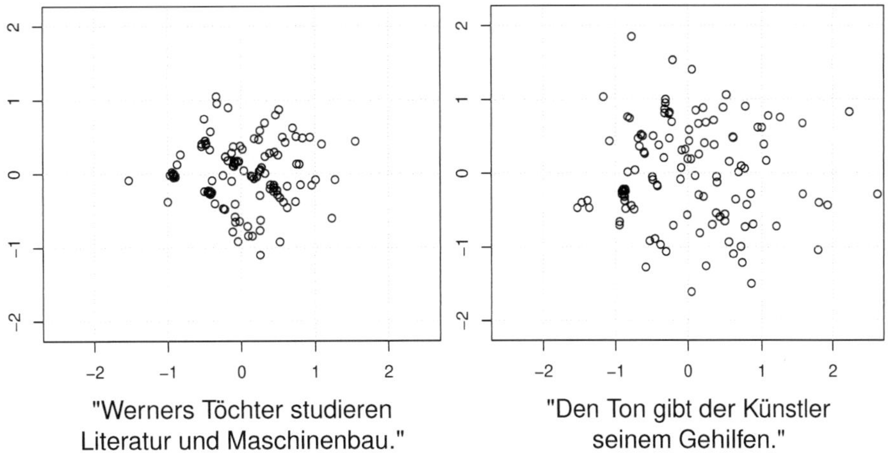

Figure 6: Two maps of scanpaths. For plotting the first two principal components of the 4-dimensional maps were used as the axes. Left, the map for the sentence that elicited the most regular scanpaths ('Wolfgang's daughters study literature and engineering') and on the right for the sentence that elicited the most irregular scanpaths ('The artist gave the clay to his apprentice'). Each point represents a scanpath that was produced by a different reader. Distances between the points reflect the dissimilarities of the corresponding scanpaths. The first sentence has canonical word order while the second has non-canonical word order and a lexical ambiguity which can lead to garden-pathing ("Ton" can mean sound or clay).

one of 230 readers read the sentence. Fig. 6 shows the maps for the following two sentences:

(4)	*Wolfgangs*	*Töchter*	*studieren*	*Literatur*	*und*	*Maschinenbau.*
	Wolfgang's	daughters	study	literature	and	engineering.

(5)	*Den*	*Ton*	*gab*	*der*	*Künstler*	*seinem Gehilfen.*
	The	clay	gave	the	artist	to his apprentice.
	'The artist gave the clay to his apprentice.'					

The first sentence has canonical word order and long words. Hence, it should elicit relatively regular scanpaths. The second sentence has non-canonical word order, contains a lexical ambiguity ("Ton" can mean clay or sound), and has short words, which should result in relatively irregular scanpaths. Looking at the maps in fig. 6, we see that the density of scanpaths is higher for the first sentence and lower for the second sentence. This follows from the fact that scanpaths for sentence (4) were more similar to each other than those recorded for sentence (5) (distance on the map reflects dissimilarity according to our Scasim measure). Thus we can use density on the map to quantify the regularity of scanpaths: if a scanpath is located in a low-density area of a map it is relatively irregular (i.e., there were few similar scanpaths). If, however, a scanpath is located in a high-density area it followed a common pattern and more regular pattern.

In order to calculate density, we again used mixture models, this time however to derive a density function for each of the 144 maps. The density scores of the scanpaths were then modeled as a function of syntactic difficulty of sentences, average word length in sentences, age of readers, and the interactions of these factors (linear mixed models, Bates, 2005). Syntactic difficulty was measured as the average surprisal (Hale, 2001) and the average retrieval cost in a sentence Lewis and Vasishth (2005). Surprisal quantifies the unexpectedness of a word given the preceding words and retrieval cost the difficulty of retrieving dependents of a word from working memory assuming temporal decay and similarity-based interference between memory items. These two measures thus capture different aspects of sentence processing. Both measures were taken from Boston et al. (2011) and added to the model as separate predictors.

All predictions were confirmed. Older readers produced more irregular scanpaths than younger readers. Sentences with short words, high surprisal, or high retrieval cost elicited more irregular scanpath patterns. Additionally, both syntactic measures interacted with age to the effect that older readers had weaker effects of syntax than younger readers. The results thus show that our scanpath measure is sensitive to effects attributable to different levels of processing. Also they show that scanpath analyses can be informative not only when the effects are relatively pronounced, as typically seen in garden-path sentences, but also when the eyes move relatively straight from left to right, that is, when the effects are relatively subtle.

How would an analysis based on traditional eyetracking measures have fared? We have not done a formal comparison but it is easy to see how, for instance, an analysis of regression probability could be problematic: a short word length and a high syntactic difficulty both increase the rate of regressions and therefore increase irregularity. The type of regression may be different, though. In the case of word length, we expect a regression back to the skipped word directly following the skip. Thus, at the short word the eyes hit a snag but that leads only to a small detour in the gaze trajectory. In the case of a syntactic obstacle, the detour may be larger—perhaps the eyes revisit earlier material for rereading? Syntax may therefore have a different impact on scanpaths than word length. Yet, this difference would not be reflected in regression probability. Of course, the difference in this particular example can be captured in other measures, e.g., total reading time, but these measures will fail to distinguish other patterns. Thus, classical eyetracking measures present a puzzle that is difficult to solve. Compared to that, our scanpath metric is a compound measure of all aspects in a scanpath. All spatial and temporal deviations from a regular reading pattern are captured and distinguishable.

5 Conclusions

Scanpaths have been in the focus of pioneering eyetracking studies in the research on reading (Frazier and Rayner, 1982) and visual scene perception (Yarbus, 1967). Nevertheless, analyses of scanpaths have not gained much traction, perhaps because of a lack of suitable methods for analyzing them. Particularly in reading research, scanpaths have not played an important role. Here, we summarized our previous work showing that scanpaths are analytically tractable and informative about the processes involved in reading. It remains to been seen how the proposed methods can be applied to other types of data such as eye movements in the visual world paradigm.

References

Bates, D. (2005). Fitting linear mixed models in R. *R News*, 5(1):27–31.

Bicknell, K. and Levy, R. (2010). A rational model of eye movement control in reading. In Hajič, J., editor, *Proceedings of the 48th Annual Meeting of the Association for Computational Linguistics*, pages 1168–1178, Uppsala, Sweden. Association for Computational Linguistics.

Bicknell, K. and Levy, R. (2011). Why readers regress to previous words: A statistical analysis. In *Proceedings of the 33rd Annual Meeting of the Cognitive Science Society*, Boston, Massachusetts. Cognitive Science Society.

Boston, M. F., Hale, J. T., Kliegl, R., Patil, U., and Vasishth, S. (2008). Parsing costs as predictors of reading difficulty: An evaluation using the Potsdam Sentence Corpus. *Journal of Eye Movement Research*, 2(1):1–12.

Boston, M. F., Hale, J. T., Vasishth, S., and Kliegl, R. (2011). Parallel processing and sentence comprehension difficulty. *Language and Cognitive Processes*, 26(3):301–349.

Brandt, S. A. and Stark, L. W. (1997). Spontaneous eye movements during visual imagery reflect the content of the visual scene. *Journal of Cognitive Neuroscience*, 9(1):27–38.

Brysbaert, M. and Vitu, F. (1998). *Word skipping: Implications for theories of eye movement control in reading*, chapter 6, pages 125–148. Elsevier, Oxford, England.

Clifton, C., Staub, A., and Rayner, K. (2007). *Eye Movements in Reading Words and Sentences*, chapter 15, pages 341–374. Elsevier Science Ltd., Amsterdam, Netherlands.

Coco, M. I. and Keller, F. (2012). Scan patterns predict sentence production in the cross-modal processing of visual scenes. *Cognitive Science*, 36(7):1204–1223.

Cristino, F., Mathôt, S., Theeuwes, J., and Gilchrist, I. D. (2010). ScanMatch: A novel method for comparing fixation sequences. *Behavior Research Methods*, 42(3):692.

Daniel, P. M. and Whitteridge, D. (1961). The representation of the visual field on the cerebral cortex in monkeys. *The Journal of Physiology*, 159:203–221.

Drieghe, D., Rayner, K., and Pollatsek, A. (2005). Eye movements and word skipping during reading revisited. *Journal of Experimental Psychology: Human Perception and Performance*, 31(5):954–969.

Engbert, R., Nuthmann, A., Richter, E. M., and Kliegl, R. (2005). Swift: A dynamical model of saccade generation during reading. *Psychological Review*, 112(4):777–813.

Fraley, C. and Raftery, A. E. (2002). Model-based clustering, discriminant analysis, and density estimation. *Journal of the American Statistical Association*, 97(458):611–632.

Fraley, C. and Raftery, A. E. (2007). MCLUST version 3 for R: Normal mixture modeling and model-based clustering. Technical Report 504, Department of Statistics University of Washington, Seattle, WA 98195-4322 USA.

Frazier, L. (1979). *On comprehending sentences: Syntactic parsing strategies*. PhD thesis, University of Connecticut, Storrs, CT.

Frazier, L. and Rayner, K. (1982). Making and correcting errors during sentence comprehension: Eye movements in the analysis of structurally ambiguous sentences. *Cognitive Psychology*, 14(2):178–210.

Hale, J. (2001). A probabilistic Earley parser as a psycholinguistic model. In Kehler, A., Levin, L., and Marcu, D., editors, *Proceedings of NAACL 2001*, pages 1–8, Morristown, NJ, USA. Association for Computational Linguistics.

Huettig, F., Rommers, J., and Meyer, A. S. (2011). Using the visual world paradigm to study language processing: A review and critical evaluation. *Acta Psychologica*, 137(2):151–171.

Jarodzka, H., Holmqvist, K., and Nyström, M. (2010). A vector-based, multidimensional scanpath similarity measure. In *Proceedings of the 2010 Symposium on Eye-Tracking Research & Applications*, pages 211–218. ACM.

Josephson, S. and Holmes, M. E. (2002). Attention to repeated images on the world-wide web: Another look at scanpath theory. *Behavior Research Methods*, 34(4):539–548.

Just, M. A. and Carpenter, P. A. (1980). A theory of reading: From eye fixations to comprehension. *Psychological Review*, 87(4):329.

Kaiser, E., T. Runner, J., S. Sussman, R., and Tanenhaus, M. K. (2009). Structural and semantic constraints on the resolution of pronouns and reflexives. *Cognition*, 112(1):55–80.

Kaplan, R. M. (1972). Augmented transition networks as psychological models of sentence comprehension. *Artificial Intelligence*, 3(1–3):77–100.

Kliegl, R., Grabner, E., Rolfs, M., and Engbert, R. (2004). Length, frequency, and predictability effects of words on eye movements in reading. *European Journal of Cognitive Psychology*, 16(1/2):262–284.

Kruskal, J. (1964). Multidimensional scaling by optimizing goodness of fit to a nonmetric hypothesis. *Psychometrika*, 29(1):1–27.

Levenshtein, V. (1966). Binary Codes Capable of Correcting Deletions and Insertions and Reversals. *Soviet Physics Doklady*, 10(8):707–710.

Lewis, R. L. and Vasishth, S. (2005). An activation-based model of sentence processing as skilled memory retrieval. *Cognitive science*, 29(3):1–45.

von der Malsburg, T., Kliegl, R., and Vasishth, S. (2012). Determinants of scanpath regularity in reading. Manuscript under revision. Available on request from the first author.

von der Malsburg, T. and Vasishth, S. (2007). A time-sensitive similarity measure for scanpaths. In *Proceedings of European Conference on Eye Movements*, Potsdam, Germany.

von der Malsburg, T. and Vasishth, S. (2011). What is the scanpath signature of syntactic reanalysis? *Journal of Memory and Language*, 65(2):109–127.

von der Malsburg, T. and Vasishth, S. (2012). Scanpath patterns in reading reveal syntactic under-specification and reanalysis strategies. *Language and Cognitive Processes*. In press. Available on request from the first author.

Mathôt, S., Cristino, F., Gilchrist, I. D., and Theeuwes, J. (2012). A simple way to estimate similarity between pairs of eye movement sequences. *Journal of Eye Movement Research*, 5(1):1–15.

Meseguer, E., Carreiras, M., and Clifton, C. (2002). Overt reanalysis strategies and eye movements during the reading of mild garden path sentences. *Memory & Cognition*, 30(4):551–561.

Mitchell, D. C., Shen, X., Green, M. J., and Hodgson, T. L. (2008). Accounting for regressive eye-movements in models of sentence processing: A reappraisal of the Selective Reanalysis hypothesis. *Journal of Memory and Language*, 59(3):266–293.

Needleman, S. B. and Wunsch, C. D. (1970). A general method applicable to the search for similarities in the amino acid sequence of two proteins. *Journal of Molecular Biology*, 48(3):443–453.

R Development Core Team (2009). *R: A Language and Environment for Statistical Computing*. R Foundation for Statistical Computing, Vienna, Austria. ISBN 3-900051-07-0.

Rayner, K. (1975). The perceptual span and peripheral cues in reading. *Cognitive Psychology*, 7(1):65–81.

Rayner, K. (1998). Eye movements in reading and information processing: 20 years of research. *Psychological Bulletin*, 124(3):372–422.

Rayner, K., Reichle, E. D., Stroud, M. J., Williams, C. C., and Pollatsek, A. (2006). The effect of word frequency, word predictability, and font difficulty on the eye movements of young and older readers. *Psychology and Aging*, 21(3):448–465.

Rovamo, J., Virsu, V., and Näsänen, R. (1978). Cortical magnification factor predicts the photopic contrast sensitivity of peripheral vision. *Nature*, 271(5640):54–56.

Salvucci, D. D. and Anderson, J. R. (2001). Automated eye-movement protocol analysis. *Human-Computer Interaction*, 16(1):39–86.

Schwarz, G. (1978). Estimating the dimension of a model. *The Annals of Statistics*, 6(2):461–464.

Vasishth, S., von der Malsburg, T., and Engelmann, F. (2012). What can eye-tracking tell us about sentence processing? *WIREs Cognitive Science*. In press.

Vitu, F. and McConkie, G. W. (2000). *Regressive saccades and word perception in adult reading.*, chapter 12, pages 301–326. Elsevier, Amsterdam, Netherlands.

Yarbus, A. L. (1967). Eye movements and vision. *Plenum*.

Predicting Word Fixations in Text with a CRF Model for Capturing General Reading Strategies among Readers

Tadayoshi Hara[1] *Daichi Mochihashi*[2] *Yoshinobu Kano*[1,3] *Akiko Aizawa*[1]
(1) National Institute of Informatics, Japan
(2) The Institute of Statistical Mathematics, Japan
(3) PRESTO, Japan Science and Technology Agency
harasan@nii.ac.jp, daichi@ism.ac.jp, {kano, aizawa}@nii.ac.jp

Abstract

Human gaze behavior while reading text reflects a variety of strategies for precise and efficient reading. Nevertheless, the possibility of extracting and importing these strategies from gaze data into natural language processing technologies has not been explored to any extent. In this research, as a first step in this investigation, we examine the possibility of extracting reading strategies through the observation of word-based fixation behavior. Using existing gaze data, we train conditional random field models to predict whether each word is fixated by subjects. The experimental results show that, using both lexical and screen position cues, the model has a prediction accuracy of between 73% and 84% for each subject. Moreover, when focusing on the distribution of fixation/skip behavior of subjects on each word, the total similarity between the predicted and observed distributions is 0.9462, which strongly supports the possibility of capturing general reading strategies from gaze data.

Title and Abstract in Japanese

人の一般的な文章理解戦略を捉えるための CRF モデルを用いた文章中の単語注視予測

人間が文章を読む際の視線行動には、正確かつ効率的に読むための様々な戦略が反映されている。しかしながら、その戦略を視線データから抽出し、自然言語処理技術に取り入れるという可能性に関しては、これまでほとんど研究されて来なかった。本研究では、この可能性を研究するための第一歩として、単語ベースの注視行動の観察を通して文章理解戦略の抽出可能性を調査する。我々は既存の視線データを用い、各単語が被験者によって注視されるかどうかを予測する条件付き確率場モデルを訓練する。実験では、語彙情報と画面位置情報を手がかりにすることで、このモデルが各被験者に対して 73%から 84%の予測精度を与えることが示される。さらに、各単語に対する被験者間の注視／スキップの分布に着目すると、予測された分布と実際に観察された分布との全体的な近似度は 0.9462 であることが示され、視線データから一般的な文章理解戦略を捉えうる可能性を強く裏付ける実験結果となっている。

Keywords: eye-tracking, gaze data, reading behavior, conditional random field (CRF).

Keywords in Japanese: 視線追跡、視線データ、読解行動、条件付き確率場 (CRF).

1 Introduction

Natural language processing (NLP) technologies have long been explored and some have approached close to satisfactory performance. Nevertheless, even for such sophisticated technologies, there are still various issues pending further improvement. For example, in parsing technologies, over 90% parsing accuracy has been achieved, yet some coordination structures or modifier dependencies are still analyzed incorrectly.

Humans, on the other hand, can deal with such issues relatively effectively. We expect that if we could clarify the mechanism used by humans, the performance of NLP technologies could be improved by incorporating such mechanisms in their systems. To clarify these mechanisms, analyzing human reading behavior is essential, while gaze data should strongly reflect this behavior. When a human reads a piece of text, especially for the first time, it is important that his/her eye movements are optimized for rapid understanding of the text. Humans typically perform this optimization unconsciously, which is reflected in the gaze data.

Eye movements while reading text have long been explored in the field of psycholinguistics (Rayner, 1998), and the accumulated knowledge of human eye movements has been reflected in various eye movement models (Reichle et al., 1998, 2003, 2006). Reinterpretation of the knowledge from an NLP perspective, however, has not been thoroughly investigated (Nilsson and Nivre, 2009, 2010; Martínez-Gómez et al., 2012). One possible reason for this could be that eye movements inevitably contain individual differences among readers as well as unstable movements caused by various external or internal factors, which make it difficult to extract general reading strategies from gaze data obtained from different readers or even from a single reader.

In this research, we explore whether this difficulty can be overcome. We aim to predict whether each word in the text is fixated by training conditional random field (CRF) models on existing gaze data (Kennedy, 2003), and then examining whether such fixation behavior can be sufficiently explained from the viewpoint of NLP-based linguistic features.

In the experiments, the trained CRF models predicted word fixations with 73% to 84% accuracy for each subject. While the accuracy does not seem high enough to explain human gaze behavior, a CRF model trained on the merged gaze data of all the subjects can predict the fixation distribution across subjects for each word with a similarity of 0.9462 to the observed distribution, which should be high enough to extract a general distribution regardless of individual differences or unstable movements in the gaze data. The experimental results also show that to capture human reading behavior correctly, both lexical and screen position features are essential, which would suggest that we need to adequately distinguish the effects of these two kinds of features on gaze data when incorporating certain strategies from gaze data into NLP technologies.

In Section 2, we discuss related work on analyzing gaze data obtained while reading text. In Section 3, we briefly explain the fundamental concepts of gaze data by introducing existing gaze data in the form of the Dundee Corpus, and also introduce the CRF model, which is trained to predict word-based fixations. In Section 4, we discuss preprocessing and observation of the Dundee Corpus in designing our model. Finally, in Sections 5 and 6, we explain how to predict word-based fixations in the corpus and analyze the performance of our model, respectively.

2 Related work

In the field of psycholinguistics, eye movements while reading text is a well established research field (Rayner, 1998), and the accumulated knowledge has resulted in various models for eye movements. E-Z Reader (Reichle et al., 1998, 2003, 2006) is one such model. The E-Z Reader was developed to explain how eye movements are generated for the target gaze data, and not to predict eye movements when reading text for the first time. These models are optimized for the target gaze data by adjusting certain parameters without including any machine learning approaches. On the other hand, the work presented in (Nilsson and Nivre, 2009) was, as the authors stated, the first work that incorporated a machine learning approach to model human eye movements. The authors predicted word-based fixations for unseen text using a transition-based model. In (Nilsson and Nivre, 2010), temporal features were also considered to predict the duration of fixations.

There are important differences between the two approaches mentioned above, other than the way in which the parameters are adjusted and the purpose of the modeling. The former approach modeled the average eye movement of the subjects, while the latter trained the model for each subject. The key point here is that the former approach attempts to generalize human eye-movement strategies, while the latter attempts to capture individual characteristics. Our final goal is not only to explain or predict human eye movements, but rather to extract from gaze data, reading strategies that can be imported into NLP technologies. Since it is not clear whether extracting individual or averaged strategies is better for this purpose, we set out to train our models to predict both word-based fixations for each subject and the total distribution of the behavior across the subjects.

An image-based approach was proposed in (Martínez-Gómez et al., 2012) to clarify the position in the text that should be fixated in order to understand the text more quickly. The authors represented words in the text as bounding boxes, and visualized each of the linguistic features of words as an image by setting the pixel values of the word-bounding boxes according to the magnitude of the feature values of the words. They then attempted to explain the target gaze data represented in the image using a linear sum of the weighted feature images. This work also incorporated screen position features of words by representing each linguistic feature in a text image, which meant that the screen position and linguistic features were considered to be strongly connected. In our models, on the other hand, these two features are described separately and then paired, since we need to exclude the contribution of screen position features when incorporating captured reading strategies into NLP technologies, where screen positions are rarely considered.

3 The target gaze data and the model used to analyze them

3.1 The Dundee Corpus

The Dundee Corpus (Kennedy, 2003) is a corpus of eye movement data obtained while reading English and French text. For each language, 20 texts from newspaper editorials (each of which contained around 2,800 words) were selected, and each of the texts was divided into 40 five-line screens containing 80 characters per line. While 10 native speakers read the texts displayed on the screen, an eye tracker was used to record the gaze points on the text every millisecond. Through their screen settings, patient calibration of the eye tracker, and post-adjustment of gaze data, the authors successfully controlled the error of each gaze point to be within a character. The gaze data included in the corpus, therefore, consisted of character-based fixations. Consecutive gaze points on a single character were reduced to a single fixation point with the combined duration (Figure 1).

Generally, an eye movement from one fixation point to another is called a *saccade*, and backward saccades are called *regressions*. In a saccade action, the human gaze usually moves several characters forward in the text, which means that some characters are not fixated. The reason for this is that humans can see and process the areas around fixated points, referred to as *peripheral fields*.

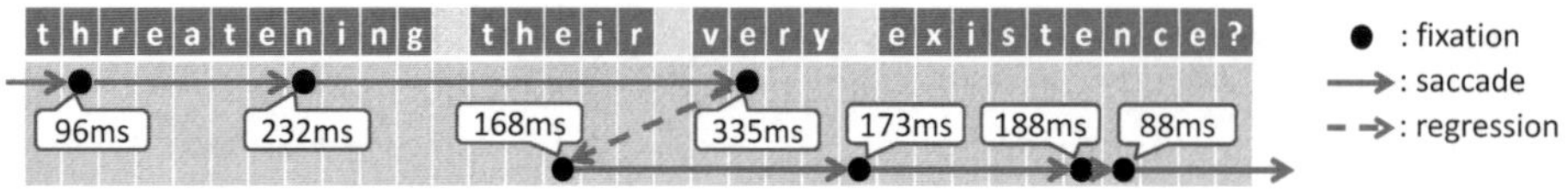

Figure 1: Character-based gaze data in the Dundee Corpus

3.2 Conditional random fields

CRFs (Lafferty et al., 2001) are a type of discriminative undirected probabilistic graphical model. Theoretically, CRFs can deal with various types of graph structures although we use CRFs for sequential labeling of whether each word is fixated. We therefore, explain CRFs with respect to sequences only, borrowing the explanation from (Sha and Pereira, 2003).

CRFs define the conditional probability distributions $p(\boldsymbol{Y}|\boldsymbol{X})$ of label sequences $\boldsymbol{Y}$ given input sequences $\boldsymbol{X}$. We assume that random variable sequences $\boldsymbol{X}$ and $\boldsymbol{Y}$ have the same length, and that the generic input and label sequences are $\boldsymbol{x} = x_1 \cdots x_n$ and $\boldsymbol{y} = y_1 \cdots y_n$, respectively. A CRF on $(\boldsymbol{X}, \boldsymbol{Y})$ is specified by a vector $\boldsymbol{f}$ of *local features* and a corresponding *weight vector* $\boldsymbol{\lambda}$. Each local feature is either a state feature $s(y, \boldsymbol{x}, i)$ or a transition feature $t(y, y', \boldsymbol{x}, i)$ where y, y' are labels, $\boldsymbol{x}$ is an input sequence, and i is an input position. Typically, features depend on the inputs around the given position, although they may also depend on global properties of the input.

The CRF's global feature vector for input sequence $\boldsymbol{x}$ and label sequence $\boldsymbol{y}$ is given by $\boldsymbol{F}(\boldsymbol{y}, \boldsymbol{x}) = \sum_i \boldsymbol{f}(\boldsymbol{y}, \boldsymbol{x}, i)$, where i ranges over the input positions. The conditional probability distribution defined by the CRF is then $p_{\lambda}(\boldsymbol{Y}|\boldsymbol{X}) = (1/Z_{\lambda}(\boldsymbol{X})) \exp \boldsymbol{\lambda} \cdot \boldsymbol{F}(\boldsymbol{Y}, \boldsymbol{X})$, where $Z_{\lambda}(\boldsymbol{x}) = \sum_{\boldsymbol{y}} \exp \boldsymbol{\lambda} \cdot \boldsymbol{F}(\boldsymbol{y}, \boldsymbol{x})$. The most likely label sequence for $\boldsymbol{x}$ is then given by $\hat{\boldsymbol{y}} = \arg\max_{\boldsymbol{y}} p_{\lambda}(\boldsymbol{y}|\boldsymbol{x}) = \arg\max_{\boldsymbol{y}} \boldsymbol{\lambda} \cdot \boldsymbol{F}(\boldsymbol{y}, \boldsymbol{x})$. In our case, $\boldsymbol{x}$ represents the words in the text and $\boldsymbol{y}$ denotes whether each word is fixated.

4 Pre-processing and observation of the Dundee Corpus

In this section, we extract first-pass word-based fixations from the Dundee Corpus as the first step in our investigation. We then observe what types of information seem to determine word fixations/skips, which will help us to design feature sets for our CRF model in Section 5.

4.1 Extraction of first-pass word-based fixations from the Dundee Corpus

As a first step toward extracting reading strategies, we focus on word-based fixations ignoring their duration information, as examined in (Nilsson and Nivre, 2009). By merging consecutive fixations within a word into a single fixation, the resolution of the gaze data is reduced from a per character to a per word basis. Even after the merging, however, considering various types of observable behaviors at a time seems too complicated for the first step. We therefore further narrow our target by excluding regressions and saccades crossing lines from the gaze data as follows.

[Step 1] Each word-fixation is dealt with according to **(i)** and **(ii)**.
  (i) Omit the fixation from the gaze data and move to the next fixation if a fixated word
    (a) is labeled "*visited*" or **(b)** is in a different line from a previously-fixated word.
  (ii) Else, allocate "*visited*" labels to the fixated word and all the preceding words in the text.
[Step 2] A sequence of gaze data is reconstructed using the remaining fixations.

For the gaze data in Figure 1, for example, character-based fixations are first merged into word-based fixations, the fixation after the regression from *very* to *their* is then ignored, and thereafter the gaze data are reconstructed as shown in Figure 2. With the data obtained from the above operation,

Figure 2: First-pass word-based fixations in the Dundee Corpus

Subject	Total no. of saccades	No. of words in word sequence skipped by saccade 0	1	2	3	4	5	6	7	…
A	31,431	17,683	8,831	3,928	777	144	30	16	8	…
B	36,248	24,669	8,900	2,118	419	106	28	3	1	…
C	37,657	26,348	9,369	1,704	168	32	16	12	3	…
D	36,570	24,560	10,044	1,750	143	40	14	10	4	…
E	32,442	18,896	9,023	3,672	755	77	16	2	1	…
F	38,982	28,561	8,859	1,351	159	36	10	3	1	…
G	38,910	28,640	8,324	1,732	160	25	13	7	2	…
H	33,910	20,540	10,068	2,807	384	78	18	8	1	…
I	36,717	24,957	9,117	2,393	216	23	8	1	0	…
J	37,738	26,479	9,297	1,774	136	32	12	2	2	…
Avg.	36,060.5	24,133.3	9,183.2	2,322.9	331.7	59.3	16.5	6.4	2.3	…
	(100.00%)	(66.91%)	(25.46%)	(6.44%)	(0.92%)	(0.16%)	(0.05%)	(0.02%)	(0.01%)	…

Table 1: Frequency of number of words in skipped sequence per subject

we can focus only on word-fixations involved in first-pass forward saccades within single lines.

4.2 Observation of skipped words in the Dundee Corpus

When observing the gaze data obtained in the previous section, we can see that for each subject many words were skipped by saccades, that is, not fixated at all. We consider that such skips would reduce the time for word-fixations and therefore lead to more effective human reading, that is, faster reading without sacrificing understanding. Here we explore this word-skip behavior in the gaze data in order to utilize the characteristics thereof to model word-fixations in the experiments.

Table 1 shows the number of saccades per subject for the 20 texts of the Dundee Corpus (second column), and classifies these saccades according to how many consecutive words the subject skipped (third column onwards). The numbers in parentheses at the bottom of the table show the ratios of the number of saccades skipping a particular number of words against the total number of saccades. According to this table, the number of saccades skipping up to three words constitutes 99.73% of the total number of saccades. Even if we omit the number of saccades that move to the next word (shown in the third column) from our calculations, the number of saccades skipping one to three words constitutes 99.18%. Based on this observation, the assumption that each saccade action skips at most three consecutive words appears to be realistic. If there is a common regularity within the skipped sequences that can determine whether a target sequence is skipped, predicting whether a target word is skipped would require lexical information on the preceding or following two words from the target word.

Table 2(a) shows the top 30 word sequences skipped by saccades in order of the number of skip times, averaged over the 10 subjects (leftmost values in the middle column). From this table, it seems that closed-class words such as determiners, prepositions, conjunctions, auxiliary verbs, and so on, are often skipped by saccades. When considering the ratio of skip times against total number of appearances of the target sequence (shown in the rightmost column), however, the frequently skipped sequences were not skipped with high frequencies. For example, *the* was skipped most often, although its skip rate was only 26.56%.

Table 2(b) shows the top 30 sequences in order of skip rates against number of appearances only for sequences that appeared ≥ 5 times in the corpus. As observed in Table 2(a), we can see that

(a) Frequently observed skips

Word sequence	# skips / # appearances	Ratio (%)
the	774.1 / 2915	26.56
of	592.9 / 1613	36.76
to	525.1 / 1442	36.41
and	430.4 / 1079	39.89
a	402.7 / 1260	31.96
in	320.7 / 934	34.34
that	201.7 / 731	27.59
is	185.8 / 625	29.73
for	146.6 / 436	33.62
The	134.9 / 319	42.29
on	121.3 / 364	33.32
as	107.2 / 348	30.80
of the	106.3 / 371	28.65
are	99.5 / 318	31.29
be	92.8 / 372	24.95
with	92.4 / 347	26.63
was	87.2 / 351	24.84
it	84.5 / 330	25.61
I	79.5 / 257	30.93
by	76.7 / 220	34.86
-	72.5 / 257	28.21
have	71.4 / 327	21.83
or	70.5 / 167	42.22
in the	68.6 / 271	25.31
at	67.4 / 220	30.64
has	64.8 / 208	31.15
from	63.1 / 215	29.35
he	59.7 / 182	32.80
but	56.7 / 170	33.35
an	51.8 / 174	29.77

(b) Sequences skipped with high rate (which appeared ≥ 5 times)

Word sequence	# skips / # appearances	Ratio (%)
His	4.8 / 8	60.00
Its	4.6 / 8	57.50
How	3.3 / 6	55.00
Of	6.7 / 13	51.54
From	3.9 / 8	48.75
A	21.7 / 46	47.17
or a	4.6 / 10	46.00
No	4.1 / 9	45.56
I'd	4.1 / 9	45.56
Ms	3.1 / 7	44.29
We	14.4 / 33	43.64
led	2.6 / 6	43.33
- in	3.0 / 7	42.86
Most	3.4 / 8	42.50
The	134.9 / 319	42.29
de	3.8 / 9	42.22
&	3.8 / 9	42.22
or	70.5 / 167	42.22
of a	30.7 / 73	42.05
Is	2.1 / 5	42.00
- is	2.5 / 6	41.67
It's	6.1 / 15	40.67
as a	20.9 / 52	40.19
'We	2.4 / 6	40.00
Those	2.4 / 6	40.00
he's	2.4 / 6	40.00
- a	3.6 / 9	40.00
He	19.6 / 49	40.00
25	2.4 / 6	40.00
and	430.4 / 1079	39.89

(c) Skipped 2 or 3 word sequences (which appeared ≥ 5 times)

Word sequence	# skips / # appearances	Ratio (%)
or a	4.6 / 10	46.00
- in	3.0 / 7	42.86
of a	30.7 / 73	42.05
- is	2.5 / 6	41.67
as a	20.9 / 52	40.19
- a	3.6 / 9	40.00
to a	13.4 / 34	39.41
and so	1.9 / 5	38.00
in a	22.9 / 64	35.78
- the	4.5 / 13	34.62
of us	3.1 / 9	34.44
In a	2.4 / 7	34.29
up a	1.7 / 5	34.00
than a	4.4 / 13	33.85
and to	2.0 / 6	33.33
to be a	2.8 / 11	25.45
many of the	0.4 / 5	8.00
to do with	0.4 / 5	8.00
is not a	0.4 / 5	8.00
would be a	0.6 / 8	7.50
it is a	0.5 / 7	7.14
is that the	0.4 / 6	6.67
to make a	0.3 / 5	6.00
have been a	0.3 / 5	6.00
it is the	0.4 / 7	5.71
that it is	0.3 / 7	4.29
as much as	0.2 / 5	4.00
in order to	0.2 / 5	4.00
because of the	0.2 / 6	3.33
in the same	0.2 / 6	3.33

Table 2: Word sequences skipped by saccades in the Dundee Corpus

closed-class words are once again in the majority while first (capitalized) words in sentences were frequently skipped, although their skip rates were, as before, not that high. Even *His* at the top of the table was skipped with a rate of only 60.00%. Table 2(c) shows the top 15 sequences based on the same criteria used in Table 2(b), but only for two- and three-word sequences. The table suggests that word sequences connecting something like NP chunks tended to be skipped, although their skip rates were not that high.

These observations suggest that target word sequences themselves seem to be related to whether they are skipped, while other factors, such as relations with surrounding words, and so on, should also be considered in skip decisions. Based on the above, we aim to capture factors for word-skip behaviors using features in the CRF models. Using CRF models trained on the gaze data, we examine how well the factors implemented as features can explain gaze behaviors.

The main purpose of this research was to capture some generality in human reading strategies from an NLP perspective. From this point of view, it is desirable to be able to explain gaze behaviors mainly using combinations of lexical information, in the normal way for NLP. For example, the width of peripheral fields and the range of saccades, which are given by human eye mechanisms, have long since been shown to control gaze behavior in psycholinguistic fields, whereas we aim to interpret them in terms of window size, word length, and so on.

Early in this section we assumed that the length of each skipped sequence is at most three words. We then attempt to predict a fixation or skip behavior for each word using lexical information on the word and the preceding and following two words, which implies a window size of five words.

Subject	No. of skipped / all words (rate)
A	20,048 / 51,501 (38.93%)
B	15,224 / 51,501 (29.56%)
C	13,817 / 51,501 (26.83%)
D	14,890 / 51,501 (28.91%)
E	19,039 / 51,501 (36.97%)
F	12,490 / 51,501 (24.25%)
G	12,570 / 51,501 (24.41%)
H	17,563 / 51,501 (34.10%)
I	14,763 / 51,501 (28.67%)
J	13,736 / 51,501 (26.67%)

Table 3: Rate of skipped words

(No. of words)

Condition for agreement	Total (rate) = Skipped + Fixated
$\geq$ 6 subjects displaying same behavior	47,320 (91.88%) = 10,109 + 37,211
$\geq$ 7 subjects displaying same behavior	39,439 (76.58%) = 6,484 + 32,955
$\geq$ 8 subjects displaying same behavior	31,855 (61.85%) = 3,473 + 28,382
$\geq$ 9 subjects displaying same behavior	24,219 (47.03%) = 1,385 + 22,834
10 (all) subjects displaying same behavior	16,313 (31.68%) = 314 + 15,999
Total words in all texts	51,501

Table 4: Agreement on gaze behavior for each word

The level of lexical information can vary, such as surface form, POS, length, probability, etc., while various combinations of these can also be considered. On the other hand, since text is displayed on a screen, optical factors must also be considered. In this research, we consider one of the most likely factors, that is, the screen position of each word. In the experiments in Sections 5 and 6, we examine the contribution of these factors by representing them as features in the CRF models.

4.3 Observation of commonality in gaze behaviors among subjects

This section investigates a method for capturing generality in gaze behavior among subjects. Using the gaze data (obtained in Section 4.1), Table 3 gives the number of words that were skipped by each subject. From this table, we can roughly see some variability in gaze behavior among subjects. Table 4 shows the degree of agreement among the subjects on whether each word is fixated or skipped. For each row, the table shows the number of words for which a minimum number of subjects displayed the same behavior. For example, words for which all the subjects displayed the same behavior comprised only 31.68% of the texts. The low agreement given in the table would suggest that it is not a good idea to specify a single common behavior for each word.

Based on this observation, we attempted instead to capture the distribution of how many subjects fixated or skipped each target word. We trained a CRF model on the merged gaze data for all 10 subjects, using the same feature set as in the model for each subject, and then used the obtained model to predict the distribution of each word in a target text.

5 Experimental settings

Based on the observation in the previous section, we examine whether word-fixations can be predicted using CRF models, which are trained on the gaze data. In this section, we explain the experimental settings mainly of features that are utilized to train CRF models.

5.1 General settings

For the experiments, we trained a CRF model on the gaze data for each subject to predict the fixation/skip behavior of the subject for each word. In addition, we also trained a CRF model on the merged data for all subjects, to predict the fixation/skip distributions of each word across the subjects. The evaluation metrics for the models are given in Section 5.3.

For gaze data, we utilized the Dundee Corpus. As introduced in Section 3.1, the Dundee Corpus consists of gaze data for 20 texts, each of which was read by 10 subjects. We then divided the data into training data, consisting of the data for 18 texts, and test data, comprising data for the remaining two texts. All the gaze data were converted into first-pass saccade data according to Section 4.1, where each word was labeled “skipped” or “fixated” for each of the subjects. In the

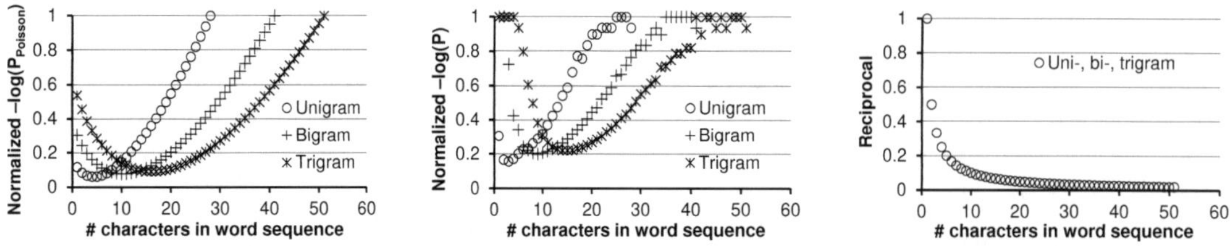

(a) L_POIS (b) L_PROB (c) L_RECI

Figure 3: Word length features

Dundee Corpus, symbols such as quotation marks, periods, and commas are concatenated with the nearest words. Considering the effect of this on gaze behavior, words in other tools were treated in the same manner. For the same reason, we left the capitalization of words unchanged.

To train the CRF models, we utilized *CRFsuite* (Okazaki, 2007) ver. 0.12. We used a sentence as an input/output unit, since many of the existing NLP technologies are based on sentence-level processing, and we intend to associate outputs of the CRF models with NLP technologies in our future work. To obtain input sentences, five 80-character lines in each screen were split into sentences using the sentence splitter implemented in the *Enju* parser (Ninomiya et al., 2007)[1]. In training the CRF models, we selected the option of maximizing the logarithm of the training data with an L1 regularization term, since this would effectively eliminate useless features, thereby highlighting those features that really contributed to capturing the gaze data. The coefficient for L1 regularization in each model was adjusted in the test data to examine to what extent we could explain the given data using our features. We next explain the features utilized for training our CRF models.

5.2 Features utilized for training CRF models

Based on the observation in Section 4.2, we set up features to capture the reading strategies. The examined features can be classified into two types: lexical features and screen position features. For each target word, we considered the features on the target word, the preceding two words, and the following two words, which implies a window size of five words. Within the window size, we considered all possible uni-, by-, and trigrams for each feature, except for **3G-F** and **3G-B**.

[Lexical features]
· **WORD**: word surface(s).
· **POS**: part(s) of speech obtained applying the POS tagger (Tsuruoka et al., 2005) to each sentence.
· **L-POIS, L-PROB, L-RECI**: information on surprisal of word length (real-value features). **L-POIS** assumes that the word length probability follows a Poisson distribution, and takes the logarithm of the probability of the target word length. The logarithmic values are normalized over the words in the texts (Figure 3(a)). **L-PROB** calculates the actual word length probability in the training data, takes the logarithm of the obtained probability, and then normalizes the logarithm (Figure 3(b)). **L-RECI** merely takes the reciprocal of the word length (Figure 3(c)). For all of the above three features, when obtaining bi- and trigrams, we summed the length of each of the words and single space characters inserted between them.
· **3G-F, 3G-B**: surprisal of a forward or backward word trigram (real-value features). We first obtained the probabilistic distribution of forward or backward trigrams by training the trigram lan-

[1] http://www.nactem.ac.uk/enju/index.html

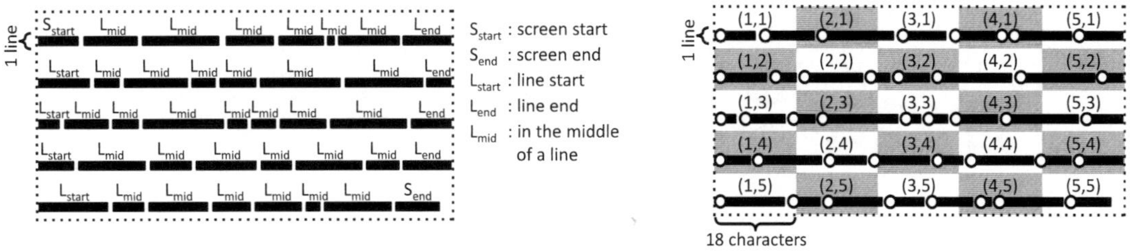

(a) LF: line- or screen-feed features

(b) SC: screen coordinate features

Figure 4: Screen position features

Subjects	A	B	C	D	E	F	G	H	I	J
# fixated words (Rate (%))	3,076 (62.67)	3,366 (68.58)	3,716 (75.71)	3,761 (76.63)	3,225 (65.71)	3,906 (79.58)	3,878 (79.01)	3,389 (69.05)	3,443 (70.15)	3,679 (74.96)
# words in test data	4,908 (100.00%)									

Table 5: Baseline rates for fixated words in the test data

guage model using SRILM (Stolcke, 2002) on the section of "Agence France-Presse, English Service" in the fourth edition of English Gigaword (Parker et al., 2009), which contains 466,718,000 words. The obtained probabilities for target trigrams were then converted into logarithmic values, and thereafter normalized over the trigrams in the texts.

[Screen position features]

· **LF**: line- or screen-feed. This examines whether the target word is at the beginning or end of a line (L_{start} / L_{end}) or the screen (S_{start} / S_{end}) (see Figure 4(a)).

· **SC**: screen coordinates. This divides each screen into 5×5 grids and examines in which grid the beginning of the word falls. Each screen in the Dundee Corpus consists of five 80-character lines, and therefore, one grid has the capacity to hold 1×16 characters (see Figure 4(b)).

5.3 Evaluation metrics and baselines

To evaluate the model trained on the gaze data for each subject, we counted the number of words in the test data for which the model correctly predicted the subject's behavior. Based on the observation that words were more often fixated than skipped for all subjects (see Table 3), we regarded the rate of fixated words in the gaze data for each subject as the baseline accuracy (see Table 5).

For the model trained on the merged data of all subjects, we first predicted the fixation/skip distributions of each word across the subjects for the test set. For each predicted distribution, the similarity based on Kullback-Leibler divergence was calculated against the distribution observed in the gaze data. Then, we took the average of the similarities over all words in the test set.

More precisely, we calculated $\exp\{-(1/|T|)\sum_{t \in T}\sum_{i} p_{i,t}\log_e(p_{i,t}/q_{i,t})\}$ where set T represents a target text in which each word $t \in T$ is identified with its position in the text. $|T|$ is accordingly the number of words in text T, $i \in \{''\text{fixated}'', ''\text{skipped}''\}$ is the label given to each $t \in T$, and $p_{i,t}$ and $q_{i,t}$ are the "fixated" / "skipped" distributions of target word t across the subjects, predicted by the CRF model and observed in the gaze data, respectively. This similarity measure returns values between $(0, 1]$; it returns 1 if the two distributions are the same. Using this similarity, we examined how well our model could capture generality in the reading strategies of all subjects.

Utilized feature types	Merged	Subjects									
		A	B	C	D	E	F	G	H	I	J
(Baseline)	.8131	62.67	68.58	75.71	76.63	65.71	79.58	79.01	69.05	70.15	74.96
WORD	.8803	68.42	70.88	76.65	80.05	70.50	79.58	79.20	70.19	72.21	77.16
POS	.8683	67.24	69.80	75.61	78.02	69.58	79.65	79.07	69.09	71.62	76.10
3G-F	.8505	64.57	68.79	75.08	75.53	66.91	79.60	79.01	67.95	69.95	75.16
3G-B	.8489	64.85	68.68	74.51	75.00	66.10	79.65	79.01	67.69	69.82	75.08
L-POIS	.8321	63.18	68.62	75.75	76.63	65.71	79.58	79.03	69.05	70.40	74.98
L-PROB	.8591	67.60	68.95	75.81	77.81	69.34	79.58	79.05	69.38	71.35	75.31
L-RECI	.8798	67.22	70.17	77.30	80.44	69.72	79.56	79.18	70.42	72.51	75.67
LF	.8663	60.96	68.58	75.65	76.83	63.12	79.58	79.01	68.38	70.44	74.96
SC	.8725	64.28	69.09	76.00	76.98	66.69	79.63	79.07	69.60	71.31	75.45
(Using all of the above)	.9462	75.24	74.37	81.05	83.94	76.51	80.48	82.62	72.98	77.69	81.11

"Merged" denotes the similarity of the distribution to the test data; "Subjects" gives the accuracy (%) of predicting word fixations/skips

Table 6: Prediction accuracy of word fixation/skip behavior (using individual features)

Utilized feature types	Merged	Subjects									
		A	B	C	D	E	F	G	H	I	J
(All individual types)	.9462	75.24	74.37	81.05	83.94	76.51	80.48	82.62	72.98	77.69	81.11
−WORD	.9460	75.06	74.67	80.75	83.99	76.51	80.50	82.38	72.84	77.51	80.58
−POS	.9457	75.02	74.33	80.91	83.99	76.24	80.34	82.46	72.72	77.71	80.81
−3G-F	.9460	75.39	74.37	80.85	83.80	76.43	80.54	82.80	72.66	77.73	81.50
−3G-B	.9463	75.04	74.49	81.03	83.88	76.47	80.48	82.58	72.84	77.73	81.48
−L-POIS	.9462	75.18	74.35	80.70	83.96	76.49	80.52	82.62	72.88	77.67	81.46
−L-PROB	.9453	75.45	74.39	80.97	83.62	76.49	80.56	82.40	72.62	77.63	81.50
−L-RECI	.9453	74.90	74.49	80.79	83.09	76.49	80.30	82.27	72.96	78.63	81.56
−LF	.9447	74.57	74.63	81.01	83.76	76.49	80.70	82.80	73.11	77.89	81.48
−SC	.9439	74.19	74.29	80.70	83.88	76.41	80.26	81.11	72.96	77.18	81.21

"Merged" denotes the similarity of the distribution to the test data; "Subjects" gives the accuracy (%) of predicting word fixations/skips

Table 7: Contribution of individual features to prediction accuracy

For the baseline of this similarity measure, we averaged over the training data the fixation/skip distributions of each word across the subjects, giving 0.8131.

6 Prediction of word-based fixation or skip behavior using CRF models

In the experiments, we first examine whether word fixation/skip behaviors in the test set can be explained using the trained CRF models. We then explore the individual contribution of each of the types of lexical and screen position features, and combinations of these features to prediction accuracy. We further observe which features are heavily weighted in the trained CRF model.

6.1 Individual contribution of each type of feature

Table 6 gives the prediction accuracy of the CRF models using each feature individually on the test data, as well as the CRF model using all of the given features. Each of the columns "A" to "J" gives the prediction accuracy for the target subject, given by the CRF models trained on training data for the target subject, while the "Merged" column gives a similarity-based evaluation of the CRF models trained on the merged gaze data of all subjects (see Section 5.3).

Using all the features, the trained CRF model gives between 0.90% and 12.57% higher accuracy than the baselines for each subject, and higher accuracy than using only individual features. The degree of contribution of each individual feature, however, seems to vary among subjects. For subjects A and E, the accuracy improvement over the baselines when using individual features is relatively higher than for other subjects. For subjects B, D, I, and J, an improvement is also observed, but this is less than for subjects A and E. For subjects F and G, on the other hand, barely any improvement is observed for all individual features. From these observations, although there

Utilized feature types	Merged	Subjects									
		A	B	C	D	E	F	G	H	I	J
(All individual types)	0.9462	75.24	74.37	81.05	83.94	76.51	80.48	82.62	72.98	77.69	81.11
−WORD, POS, 3G-F/-B	0.9437	74.53	74.39	80.52	83.68	75.94	80.42	82.23	72.82	77.63	80.56
−L-POIS/-PROB/-RECI	0.9353	73.63	73.98	80.38	82.86	75.59	80.22	82.09	72.58	77.53	81.03
−all lexical features	0.8748	64.61	68.97	75.86	76.87	66.40	79.60	79.07	69.27	71.03	75.45
−LF	0.9447	74.57	74.63	81.01	83.76	76.49	80.70	82.80	73.11	77.89	81.48
−SC	0.9439	74.19	74.29	80.70	83.88	76.41	80.26	81.11	72.96	77.18	81.21
−LF, SC	0.8940	68.93	70.90	77.49	81.09	71.11	79.54	79.67	70.48	72.84	78.26

"Merged" denotes the similarity of the distribution to the test data; "Subjects" gives the accuracy (%) of predicting word fixations/skips

Table 8: Contribution of lexical (upper part) and screen position (lower part) features to prediction

are individual differences in the degree of improvement among subjects, it seems that some of the characteristics of word-fixation behavior can be captured using our features. However, the 72% to 84% prediction accuracy obtained using all individual features is not high enough to adequately explain each subject's behavior. This is discussed further in Section 6.5.

For the CRF models trained on the merged gaze data of all subjects ("Merged" column), on the other hand, each of the individual features drastically improves the distribution similarity to the test data, and when using all features, the distribution similarity is 0.9462, which is an improvement of 0.1331 over the baseline similarity. This similarity bodes well in terms of our expectation that this CRF model can explain some generality on word-fixation behavior across all subjects.

When we go back to the prediction for each subject, each of **WORD**, **POS**, **L-PROB**, and **L-RECI** individually seem to be able to capture some characteristics in the gaze data, while **L-POIS** and the screen position features **LF** and **SC** do not improve the prediction accuracy that much. Table 7 examines the contribution of each individual feature to prediction accuracy, by training CRF models using all feature types except the target feature type. The table seems to show that removing the respective individual feature does not lead to a noticeable decrease in accuracy. This would suggest that each individual feature is complemented by the remaining features.

6.2 Contribution of lexical and screen position features

In order to explore the complementary characteristics of feature types, we start by focusing on the feature classification given by our definition: lexical and screen position features. Table 8 examines the contribution of lexical and screen position features to prediction accuracy. By removing all lexical features, that is, using only screen position features **LF** and **SC** (see "−all lexical features" row), the distribution similarity drops drastically by 0.0714, and prediction accuracy for each subject also decreases by between 0.88% and 10.63%. We observe similar characteristics by removing all screen position features; distribution similarity drops by 0.0522 (see "−**LF**, **SC**" row), while prediction accuracy for each subject also decreases by between 0.94% and 6.31%.

These observations suggest that both the lexical features and screen position features capture certain information that can only be captured by those features. In addition, the prediction accuracy obtained by removing all lexical features is similar to the baseline accuracy, regardless of the remaining screen position features. This would suggest that screen position features work well only in conjunction with lexical features. In other words, humans do not seem to be able to decide whether they fixate a word solely based on the word position.

The "−**WORD**, **POS**, **3G-F/-B**," and "−**L-POIS/-PROB/-RECI**" rows in the table show that removing either the features on word length surprisal or all lexical features other than these does

Utilized feature types	Merged	Subjects									
		A	B	C	D	E	F	G	H	I	J
Baseline	.8131	62.67	68.58	75.71	76.63	65.71	79.58	79.01	69.05	70.15	74.96
All individual types (AIT)	.9462	75.24	74.37	81.05	83.94	76.51	80.48	82.62	72.98	77.69	81.11
WORD, POS	.8805	68.58	70.64	76.55	79.97	70.64	79.60	79.18	69.89	72.07	76.81
WORD∗POS,WORD,POS	.8802	68.56	70.60	76.67	80.26	70.74	79.60	79.18	69.99	72.00	76.87
AIT, WORD∗POS	.9461	75.26	74.31	80.91	84.01	76.59	80.48	82.58	72.90	77.63	81.38
LF, SC	.8748	64.61	68.97	75.86	76.87	66.40	79.60	79.07	69.27	71.03	75.45
LF∗SC, LF, SC	.8750	64.98	69.01	75.92	76.85	66.50	79.60	79.01	69.32	71.03	75.45
AIT, LF∗SC	.9463	75.18	74.71	80.83	84.01	76.57	80.44	82.60	72.84	77.85	81.46
WORD, LF	.9322	73.08	73.61	80.11	82.76	75.49	80.64	80.48	72.62	77.24	80.50
WORD∗LF, WORD, LF	.9336	73.43	73.78	80.15	83.01	76.08	80.70	80.46	72.70	77.28	80.46
AIT, WORD∗LF	.9470	75.04	74.23	80.97	83.92	76.69	80.44	82.72	72.90	77.67	81.72
WORD, SC	.9328	73.02	73.92	80.56	82.93	75.71	80.75	82.19	73.19	77.26	81.05
WORD∗SC, WORD, SC	.9333	72.98	73.90	80.58	82.95	75.86	80.73	82.21	73.17	77.44	80.99
AIT, WORD∗SC	.9468	75.35	74.47	80.73	83.96	76.65	80.50	82.62	72.82	77.77	81.48
POS, LF	.9187	72.09	72.94	78.93	80.79	74.65	79.50	79.93	71.35	76.10	78.93
POS∗LF, POS, LF	.9201	73.11	73.08	78.79	80.93	75.26	79.16	79.56	71.31	76.14	79.03
AIT, POS∗LF	.9475	75.06	74.71	80.62	83.99	76.77	80.54	82.46	72.90	77.75	81.52
POS, SC	.9190	72.39	73.08	79.30	80.93	75.06	79.73	80.73	71.84	76.43	79.60
POS∗SC, POS, SC	.9196	72.56	73.04	79.69	80.97	75.08	79.75	80.75	71.84	76.49	79.60
AIT, POS∗SC	.9473	75.18	74.71	80.68	83.99	76.63	80.46	82.64	72.76	77.79	81.09
AIT, all combination	.9481	74.96	74.61	80.66	83.94	76.63	80.54	82.64	72.98	77.77	81.28

"Merged" denotes the similarity of the distribution to the test data; "Subjects" gives the accuracy (%) of predicting word fixations/skips

Table 9: Prediction accuracy of word fixation/skip behavior (using combined features)

not bring about a serious decline in prediction accuracy. Considering that lexical features other than the word length features, such as **WORD**, can implicitly capture a great deal of information on word length, most of the lexical information affecting word fixations/skips seems to be word length surprisal. The "−**LF**" and "−**SC**" rows in the table, on the other hand, show that removing either screen coordinate features or line-/screen-feed features does not bring about a serious decline in prediction accuracy. Considering that most of the line-/screen-feed information is implicitly contained in the screen coordinate information, most of the screen position information affecting word fixations/skips seems to be whether a target word is at the beginning or end of a line/screen.

6.3 Contribution of combined features

We also considered combinations of two feature types. Table 9 shows the contribution of each combination of features to prediction accuracy. In the table, **A∗B** represents the combination of feature types **A** and **B**, which means that this combined feature is fired only when both **A** and **B** are fired. Some feature types are real-value features, and cannot easily be combined with other feature types. We therefore, omitted the real-value features as candidates for combination. When using each combined feature, we also added the respective individual features for smoothing.

From the table, we can see that adding each of the combined features barely contributes to any accuracy improvement. Even when using all the individual and combined features (see the bottom row of the table), the improvement over using only all the individual features is barely noticeable. These observations seem to imply that combining the features does not capture any extra information than when using the features separately. Owing to a lack of gaze data, these results may be misleading, and further investigation would be required in order to continue this discussion.

6.4 Observation of heavily weighted features

From the heavily weighted features in the CRF model, we observed which features were regarded as important for explaining the gaze data. Table 10 shows the heavily weighted features in the CRF

Features (for fixations)	Weight	Features (for fixations)	Weight	Features (for skips)	Weight
L-PROB[0]	5.7808	L-RECI[-1]	0.1651	L-RECI[0]	2.0020
LF[0]= L_{end}	1.3306	SC[-2,-1]=(5,4),(5,4)	0.1639	L-POIS[+1]	0.2691
LF[0]= L_{start}	1.3210	LF[-1,0]= L_{mid}, L_{end}	0.1519	Beginning of sentence	0.2657
LF[0]= S_{end}	1.2605	SC[+2]=(1,5)	0.1454	End of sentence	0.2071
L-POIS[-1,0]	1.2218	SC[+1,+2]=(1,3),(1,3)	0.1347	POS[-1]=_COLON_	0.2023
L-PROB[-1]	0.7899	SC[0,+1,+2]=(5,3),(5,3),(1,4)	0.1299	WORD[0]=it's	0.1904
L-RECI[-2,-1]	0.5393	WORD[-1]=But	0.1284	WORD[-1]=-	0.1829
SC[+1]=(1,5)	0.4001	SC[-2,-1]=(5,1),(5,1)	0.1258	WORD[-1]=I	0.1793
LF[+1]= L_{start}	0.3422	LF[-1]= L_{end}	0.1248	LF[-2,-1,0]= L_{mid}, L_{mid}, L_{mid}	0.1756
LF[0,+1]= L_{end}, L_{start}	0.3422	LF[-1,0]= L_{end}, L_{start}	0.1248	L-PROB[-1,0]	0.1716
LF[0,+1]= L_{start}, L_{mid}	0.3265	LF[0,+1]= S_{end}, S_{start}	0.1232	WORD[0]=than	0.1599
SC[+1]=(1,3)	0.2987	LF[+1]= S_{start}	0.1232	LF[0,+1]= L_{mid}, L_{mid}	0.1584
SC[+1]=(1,4)	0.2776	SC[+2]=(1,2)	0.1182	WORD[0]=that	0.1493
L-PROB[-2,-1,0]	0.2310	SC[+2]=(1,3)	0.1146	LF[0,+1,+2]= L_{mid}, L_{mid}, L_{mid}	0.1463
3G-F[-2,-1,0]	0.2090	LF[-2]= L_{mid}	0.1092	WORD[0]=and	0.1452
SC[0]=(5,5)	0.1867	SC[0,+1]=(5,5),(1,1)	0.1079	WORD[-1]=of	0.1289
SC[+1,+2]=(1,1),(1,1)	0.1832	POS[0]=CD	0.1047	WORD[-1,0]=as, a	0.1271
SC[-1]=(5,5)	0.1721	SC[-1]=(5,4)	0.1029	WORD[0]=from	0.1267
SC[+1,+2]=(1,2),(1,2)	0.1718	POS[0,+1]=NN, NNS	0.1014	WORD[0]=which	0.1235
SC[+1]=(1,2)	0.1695	SC[-2,-1]=(5,5),(5,5)	0.1012	SC[-1,0,+1]=(1,1),(1,1),(1,1)	0.1224
SC[+1,+2]=(1,4),(1,4)	0.1660	SC[0,+1]=(1,4),(1,4)	0.1006	LF[0]= L_{mid}	0.1157

Table 10: Features that were heavily weighted in the "Merged" model using all individual features

model that was trained using all individual features on the merged training data of all subjects. The left and right tables show the features weighted for fixations and skips, respectively. A number in square brackets [ ] represents a word whose feature was captured, and identified with an offset from a target word. A sequence of two or three numbers in [ ] represents bi- or trigram features.

The tables suggest that surprisal based on word length probability and the reciprocal word length of a target word (**L-PROB[0]** and **L-RECI[0]**, respectively) have a large influence on whether subjects fixate or skip the word, respectively. For **L-PROB[0]**, according to Figure 3(b), longer words tend to give greater surprisal. This may be because the longer length possibly suggests that the word is a content word and sometimes even an unknown word. In addition, it may be possible that a longer word cannot be skipped easily by a single saccade. The heavy weight for fixations thus seems reasonable. For **L-RECI[0]**, a large value for the reciprocal word length means that the word length is short, and a shorter length possibly suggests that the word is a functional word or easily skipped by a single saccade. The weight for skips thus seems reasonable. From the viewpoint of the human eye mechanism, these features would have been fired without a fixation on a target word, using information on the word obtained by peripheral fields of the eyes or guessed from surrounding information.

For **WORD** features, most of the heavily weighted features are for skips and on target words (**WORD[0]**) that belong to a closed-class, such as *than*, *from*, and *which*. These words are not content words and tend to be short, and therefore were likely weighted heavily for skips. On the other hand, **WORD[-1]=But** was heavily weighted for fixations. The reason for this may be that when a sentence starts with *But*, it attracts the reader's interest to focus on the next word.

For **SC** features, almost all of the heavily weighted features were located in the leftmost (1,*) or rightmost (5,*) coordinates, which is consistent with our analysis in Section 6.2. Many of these features were weighted for fixations for the simple reason that the next word was in the leftmost coordinate (**SC[+1]=(1,*)**), which would mean that subjects tended to fixate last words in a line before their linefeed eye movements. **SC[0]=(5,*)** with conditions similar to **SC[+1]=(1,*)** were not weighted that highly, probably because the first character of the last word in a line does not always appear in position (5,*).

6.5 Discussion on the experimental results

The experimental results in Section 6 show that the CRF model trained for each subject does not have high prediction accuracy. When we analyzed the prediction errors, we found many long spans in the gaze data where all words were fixated. The subjects seem to have read the spans very precisely, which differed from the behavior displayed in other areas. It is natural that subjects do not maintain the same level of concentration or understanding throughout a text, yet our model was not able to capture this. We believe that this is the main reason why the CRF model for each subject does not exhibit high prediction accuracy. This issue will be addressed in our future work.

On the other hand, the experimental results also suggest that we can predict the distribution of fixation/skip behavior of each word across subjects with very high similarity to the gaze data, regardless of individual differences among subjects (see Table 4) and the above unstable movements in gaze data. This would imply the possibility of capturing and explaining generality in human reading strategies from an NLP perspective.

It should also be noted that our results also depend on the preprocessing of the gaze data in Section 4.1. The authors in (Nilsson and Nivre, 2009) also used the Dundee Corpus, and trained and examined their model to predict word-based fixation behavior for each subject. Similar to our method, they applied some preprocessing to the gaze data to remove irregular eye movements, whereas, unlike our case, they also took regressions and revisits as well as first-pass forward saccades into consideration. Since the experimental settings differed, we cannot directly compare the prediction accuracy of our results with those in (Nilsson and Nivre, 2009). However, considering that our baselines seem to be higher than those in (Nilsson and Nivre, 2009), we could say that our additional preprocessing simplified the problem and made the gaze behavior easier to capture.

We found that both lexical features and screen position features contributed to explaining the gaze data. Our final goal is to obtain some reading strategies from the gaze data, which can then be imported into NLP technologies. Considering this goal, we need to remove the screen position factors from the gaze data, since most NLP technologies consider sentence-based processing without any position information. The experimental results suggest that combined features of screen position and lexical information do not capture any extra characteristics. If this is true, we may be able to separate the two factor types without considering their mutual interaction.

Conclusion

In this research, we examined the possibility of extracting reading strategies by observing word-based fixation behavior. We trained CRF models on gaze data to predict the gaze behavior of each subject and the distribution of gaze behavior across all subjects. Using lexical and screen position features, the CRF models could predict word fixation/skip behaviors for each subject with 73% to 84% accuracy as well as the distribution of word fixation/skip behaviors across the subjects with a 0.9462 similarity to the original gaze data.

In our future work, we would like to collect gaze data on specific linguistic phenomena, such as coordination and prepositional attachment, and then attempt to extract some general reading strategies from this gaze data. Having achieved this, we aim to import the obtained strategies into NLP technologies such as parsing, to realize further progress in these fields.

Acknowledgments

This research was partially supported by "Transdisciplinary Research Integration Center, Japan", "Kakenhi, MEXT Japan [23650076]" and "JST PRESTO".

References

Kennedy, A. (2003). *The Dundee Corpus [CD-ROM]*. School of Psychology, The University of Dundee.

Lafferty, J. D., McCallum, A., and Pereira, F. C. N. (2001). Conditional random fields: Probabilistic models for segmenting and labeling sequence data. In *Proceedings of the Eighteenth International Conference on Machine Learning*, ICML '01, pages 282–289, San Francisco, CA, USA. Morgan Kaufmann Publishers Inc.

Martínez-Gómez, P., Hara, T., Chen, C., Tomita, K., Kano, Y., and Aizawa, A. (2012). Synthesizing image representations of linguistic and topological features for predicting areas of attention. In *Proceedings of the 12th Pacific Rim International Conference on Artificial Intelligence (PRICAI)*, pages 93–101, Kuching, Sarawak, Malaysia.

Nilsson, M. and Nivre, J. (2009). Learning where to look: Modeling eye movement in reading. In *Proceedings of the Thirteenth Conference on Computational Natural Language Learning (CoNLL)*, pages 93–101, Boulder, Colorado. Association for Computational Linguistics.

Nilsson, M. and Nivre, J. (2010). Towards a data-driven model of eye movement control in reading. In *Proceedings of the 2010 Workshop on Cognitive Modeling and Computational Linguistics*, pages 63–71, Uppsala, Sweden. Association for Computational Linguistics.

Ninomiya, T., Matsuzaki, T., Miyao, Y., and Tsujii, J. (2007). A log-linear model with an n-gram reference distribution for accurate HPSG parsing. In *Proceedings of IWPT 2007*. Prague, Czech Republic.

Okazaki, N. (2007). CRFsuite: a fast implementation of Conditional Random Fields (CRFs).

Parker, R., Graff, D., Kong, J., Chen, K., and Maeda, K. (2009). English Gigaword Fourth Edition. LDC2009T13.

Rayner, K. (1998). Eye movements in reading and information processing: 20 years of research. *Psychological Bulletin*, 124(3):372–422.

Reichle, E. D., Pollatsek, A., Fisher, D. L., and Rayner, K. (1998). Toward a model of eye movement control in reading. *PSYCHOLOGICAL REVIEW*, 105(1):125–157.

Reichle, E. D., Pollatsek, A., and Rayner, K. (2006). E-Z Reader: A cognitive-control, serial-attention model of eye-movement behavior during reading. *Cogn. Syst. Res.*, 7(1):4–22.

Reichle, E. D., Rayner, K., and Pollatsek, A. (2003). The E-Z reader model of eye-movement control in reading: Comparisons to other models. *Behavioral Brain Science*, 26(4):445–476.

Sha, F. and Pereira, F. (2003). Shallow parsing with conditional random fields. In *Proceedings of the 2003 Conference of the North American Chapter of the Association for Computational Linguistics on Human Language Technology - Volume 1*, NAACL '03, pages 134–141, Stroudsburg, PA, USA. Association for Computational Linguistics.

Stolcke, A. (2002). SRILM – An Extensible Language Modeling Toolkit. In *Proc. Int. Conf. Spoken Language Processing (ICSLP 2002)*.

Tsuruoka, Y., Tateishi, Y., Kim, J.-D., Ohta, T., McNaught, J., Ananiadou, S., and Tsujii, J. (2005). Developing a robust part-of-speech tagger for biomedical text. In *Advances in Informatics - 10th Panhellenic Conference on Informatics*, volume LNCS 3746, pages 382–392, Volos, Greece. ISSN 0302-9743.

A heuristic-based approach for systematic error correction of gaze data for reading

Abhijit Mishra Michael Carl Pushpak Bhattacharya
(1) Indian Institute Of Technology, Bombay
(2)CRITT, Copenhagen Business School
(3) Indian Institute Of Technology, Bombay

abhijitmishra@cse.iitb.ac.in, mc.isv@cbs.dk, pb@cse.iitb.ac.in

ABSTRACT

In eye-tracking research, temporally constant deviations between users' intended gaze location and location captured by eye-samplers are referred to as systematic error. Systematic errors are frequent and add a lot of noise to the data. It also takes a lot of time and effort to manually correct such disparities. In this paper, we propose and validate a heuristic-based technique to reduce such errors associated with gaze fixations by shifting them to their true locations. This technique is exclusively applicable for reading tasks where the visual objects (characters) are placed on a grid in a sequential manner; which is often the case in psycholinguistic studies.

KEYWORDS: EYE-TRACKING, FIXATION CORRECTION, GAZE DATA MANIPULATION, SYSTEMATIC ERROR

---

1 Introduction

In psycholinguistic studies, eye tracking experiments have often been conducted to study the human way of analysing and synthesizing text. During reading, eye movement significantly relates to the cognitive load on participants. So, analysing gaze data is useful in proving/disproving hypotheses and extracting features for training and tuning machines. But eye trackers, after all, have certain limitations and they exhibit error in capturing gaze points of individuals. Such errors could be classified into variable and systematic errors (Harnof and Halverson, 2002). Variable error is nothing but dispersed gaze-points around the intended fixation which indicate lack of precision of eye-trackers. Systematic error, on the other hand, is the drift between the gaze-point locations captured by the eye-trackers and the intended fixation. It may be caused by imperfect calibration, head movement, astigmatism and other sources (LC Technologies, 2000). With the advent of sophisticated eye-trackers (Tobii, SR Research Eyelink etc.) it has been possible to reduce variable errors. But yet there is still a demand of tools and techniques to handle systematic errors which often imposes adverse impact on gaze-point analysis.

Various methods have been proposed to handle systematic error associated with fixations. Abrams and Jonides (1988) and Juhasz et.al (2006) proposed recalibration in the course of experiment which may not be applicable for linguistic analysis since such interruptions would reduce the quality of task. For example: during translation process studies participants cache contextual evidences in their short term memory, which could be lost by such interruptions.

Hornof and Halverson (2002) introduced Required Fixation Location (RFL) technique in which they identify RFLs i.e some points on the screen which indicates the actual fixation of the candidates at a specified time. In some of the experiments they record RFLs by asking participants to place the mouse cursor over the objects they were looking at. Then they measure the discrepancies between RFLs and fixations recorded by eye-trackers and shift the fixations to the true locations. This method is not very useful where one cannot ask the user to indicate RFLs. For example, during translation studies the participant might be busy typing the translations and reading the text simultaneously. Similar is the case with annotation tasks where the user has to read and annotate a text.

The Gaze to Word Mapping (GWM) modules introduced by Špakov, (2007) is a heuristic based approach. The underlying algorithm does not make a simplistic link between the x-y coordinates of a fixation and the location of a word on the monitor, but rather tries to account for certain documented effects, closely resembling to our technique. While is it quite reasonable to believe that participants tilt towards the end of reading lines; it doesn't clearly show us a way to determine the line which the participant is looking at; given initial few fixations are nonlinear in nature. Our algorithm tries to overcome this by introducing a scoring function which guesses which line a participant is focusing on; given N initial non-linear/linear fixations starting at time T.

The Mode-of-disparities error correction technique proposed by Zhang and Hornof (2011) is useful when the visual objects are arranged in an irregular manner but fails when objects are placed on a grid such as placing a paragraph for reading.

Intuitively, for reading and writing tasks vertical displacement of fixations contribute more to the noise than that of horizontal. So in this article, we focus more on vertical directional adjustment.

Initially, before processing fixations, a set of virtual horizontal lines are drawn by joining the centre coordinates of character belonging to the respective textual lines. Fixations are extracted from the noisy data and stored sequentially in a temporal order[1]. Then they are processed and corrected in three stages. In first stage, fixations are shifted to lie on the nearest virtual lines. In the second stage transient fixations are corrected. Finally, participant's Reading Line (RL) is predicted and deviating fixations are shifted to the corresponding RLs.

This technique is applied on the Translation Process Research (TPR) database (Carl, 2012) recorded by Tobii eye-tracker using Translog-II (Carl 2012) software. Then validation is done across manually corrected fixations. Qualitative analysis is done by replaying the recorded and corrected data in Translog. In all the cases we have assumed left to right reading and writing but the technique could be slightly modified to support for languages adopting Arabic scripts.

2 Heuristics for Fixation Correction

In order to hand code rules for fixation correction, we have extensively studied the fixation sequences in TPR database. The database contains more than 450 recordings for translation, post-editing and reading experiments in 7 languages and are collected over last 5 years by a following a systematic initial experimental setup (Carl, M. and Jakobsen A.L. 2009); the eye-tracker used being Tobii, a remote eye-tracker. However, this does not bias our heuristics since many of the psycholinguistic experiments involving reading and writing tend to follow similar set-up. Moreover, other state of the art remote eye-trackers (such as SR research, SMI vision) report same or more accuracy as Tobii.

Fixations in the recorded data are corrected in three phrases as described below.

2.1 Shifting fixations to the nearest line

First of all, recorded fixations could be dispersed over the screen whereas the intended fixation should only possibly lie on visual objects such as characters. A fixation lying on the blank space between two lines is nothing but an indication of error. So the first step is to shift the fixations vertically to the nearest line. To come up with discrete lines we have taken the cursor coordinates of each character in a line and joined them to draw a virtual line. Figure 1 illustrates a set of virtual lines going through the text. These lines serve as Reading Lines (RLs) in the later processing stages.

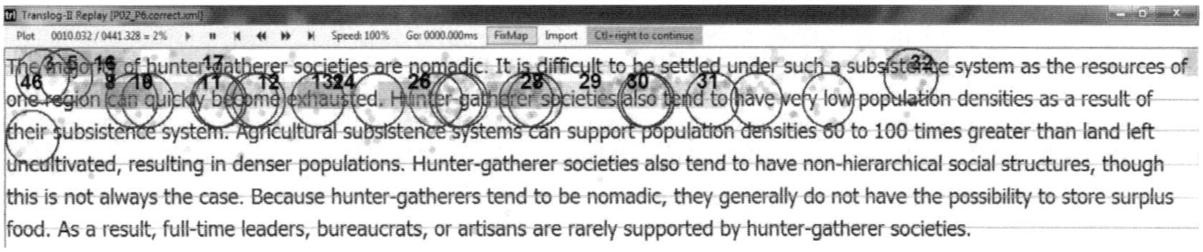

FIGURE 1 – Shifting fixations to nearest virtual lines

[1] Fixation sequencing is done on the basis of time of occurrence of the fixations. For exemple, if we say a particular fixation (say F2) follows/precedes another fixation (F1), we mean, F1 occurs sooner/later than F2 even if F2 appears to the left/right of F1 co-ordinate wise.

Figure 1 is a screen dump of Translog II, The orange lines represent virtual lines (Reading Lines). The red and green dots represent gaze samples of left and right eyes and blue circles represent fixations.

Sometimes, shifting fixations to the nearest virtual line is not enough. Upon closely looking at figure-1, one would predict that the participant is trying to read line1. But after shifting the fixations most of the fixations fall on line2.

After this step, it becomes easy to obtain systematic patterns which reduces the randomness and hence, the number of rules to be used for correction.

2.2 Discarding transient fixations

Transient Fixations (TFs) are very short duration fixations which occur in between two fixations falling nearer to each other (on the same line or just a line apart) and located far away from each of them. In other words, upon joining three fixations if we observe a spike and the tip of the spike is a short duration fixation, it is said to be transient. Figure 1 illustrates one TF.

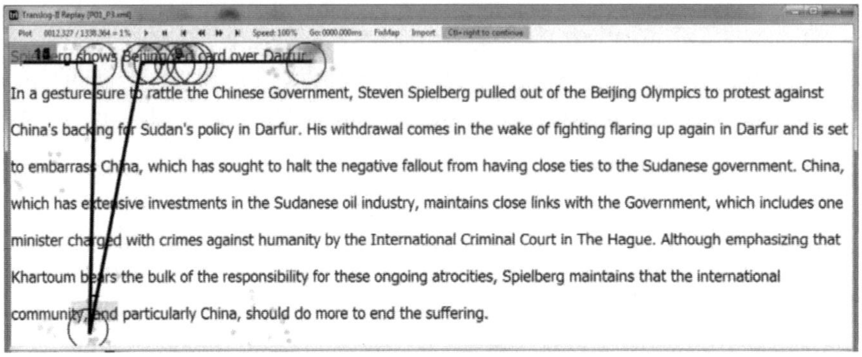

FIGURE 2 – Transient Fixations

Figure 2 shows one transient fixations. Upon joining 3 consecutive fixations involving one TF, we observe a spike.

In some studies, we do not need TFs to be present in our data as the fixation count un-necessarily grows on account of TFs. Transient fixation may also add noise to the data in some cases where, for example, fixation count for a region is a part of our study. Suppose, for our translation studies if we want to count fixations in source text window (src) and target text window (tgt) during an interval of 20 seconds and a lot of transient fixations fall on tgt, the distribution will be completely different from that of if we discard transient fixations. Such cases would require discarding TFs.

2.3 Correcting continuous abnormalities in fixation sequences

In this stage we try to predict the Reading Line (RL) of the participant at a specified time period and try to shift way-ward fixations within that time period to the corresponding RL. For instance, consider the case where the user starts reading the text from left to right and the eye-tracker records F fixations within the timespan of T. After shifting those fixations to the nearest lines, it is observed that first N out of the F fixations lie on line1. Here we can, to some extent, believe that the RL for the participant for the timespan T is line1. Now suppose the rest (F-N) fixations lie on line2 and the X co-ordinate of these fixations are greater than those of first N fixations. In this case, it is unlikely that the RL of the user has changed from line 1 to line2. Hence those (F-N) fixations have to be relocated to line1.

Assuming that the initial calibration is perfect enough for a particular experiment session and the line spacing width significant (which is often the set up in linguistic studies) , it is reasonable to believe that most of the first N (co-ordinate wise) fixations decide the RLs. The intuition behind such an assumption is that, if the participant is reading from left to right, after reading certain words from left, there will be a gradual head movement and tilting which might contribute to shifting of fixations to the next/previous line.

The value of N is decided by taking samples from the recorded data and observing it by replaying the recordings. It is highly possible that the first N fixations could be distributed amongst different lines; each being a candidate RL. In such cases we infer the RL by ranking the candidates as follows

$$RL = \text{argmax}_{r\in R} \sum_{f\in firstN} \sum_{r\in R} (\delta_r\,(f.Y) \times dur(f))$$

where R is the set of RLs, δ is Dirac Delta function and dur(f) is duration of fixation f

The first part of the summation represents fixation frequency distribution amongst the RIs. The intuition behind taking such a function is that during reading/writing, fixation duration and frequency are measurable factors providing evidences regarding participant's attention. The rationale behind taking Dirac Delta is that one particular fixation at time T could lie only on one Reading Line.

If the scores of two potential RLs match, RL is assigned to the line having maximum fixation. If that still matches, random assignment has to be done. Once the RL for a particular time period has been detected, the following two types of deviations are corrected.

Type A: This is a case when the user tries to read M^{th} line from left to right. A few fixations (say P) lie on line M spatially followed by a number of fixations (say F) on line M+1. The x-coordinates of those F fixations are greater than those of P. In such cases those F fixations are shifted upward to line M unchanging x-coordinates. (Figure 3 Type A)

Type B: Here, the user tries to read M^{th} line from left to right. A few fixations (say P) lie on line M spatially followed by a number of fixations (say F) on line M-1. The x-coordinates of those F fixations are greater than those of P. In such cases those F fixations are shifted downward to line M unchanging x-coordinates. (Figure 3 Type B)

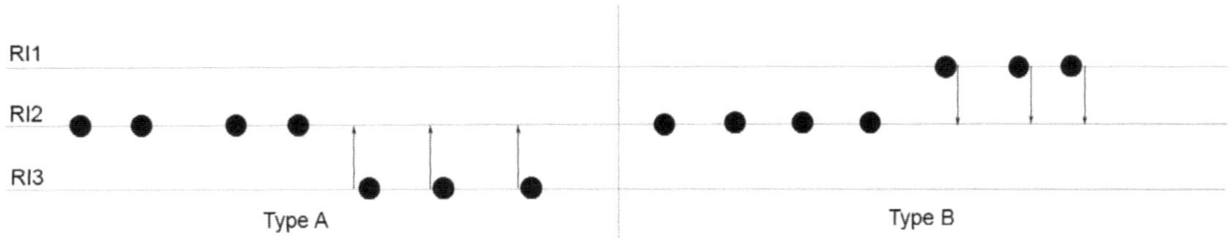

FIGURE 3 – Type A and Type B deviations

3 Algorithm

```
correctFixations (N, loggedData):
        fixationSet := extractFixations(loggedData)
        fixationSet = sortByTimeOfOccurrence (fixationSet)
        RL_Set := extractDistinctYCoordinate(loggedData)
        Foreach fixation in fixationSet:
                Re-assign the y-coordinate of the fixation to that of the closest RL
        correctTransientFixations (fixationSet)
        correctAbnormalities (fixationSet,N,RL_Set)
        Update logged data with fixationSet
        return
correctTransientFixations (fixationSet):
        averageFixationDuration := ComputeAvarageFixationDuration(fixationSet)
        Foreach fixation in fixationSet:
        IF previousFixation doesn't exist OR nextFixation doesn't exist
                Continue
        IF abs(previousFixation.Y-nextFixation.Y) << abs(previousFixation.Y -fixation.Y)
                        AND fixation.duration  << averageFixationDuration)
                Delete fixation from fixationSet
correctAbnormalities (fixationSet,N,RL_Set):
        startingPoint := 1
        firstN: = selectNFixations(fixationSet, startingPoint,N)
        RL:= getRLWithMaximumScore(firstN,RL_Set)
        X: = getLargestXCoordinate(firstN,RL)
        targetSet: = setDifference(fixationSet,firstN)
        Foreach fixation in targetSet -:
                startingPoint+=1
                L1 = getLineNumber(fixation.Y)
                L2 = getLineNumber (RL)
                IF previousFixation doesn't exist OR nextFixation doesn't exist
                        Continue
                IF (previousFixation.X > fixation.X and previousFixation.X>nextFixation.X)
                        RL = getRLWithMaximumScore(firstN,RL_Set)
                        X = getLargestXCoordinate(firstN,RL)
                        targetSet = setDifference(fixationSet,firstN)
                        Continue
                IF (abs(L2-L1)==1 and fixation.X >X)
                        fixation.Y = RL
```

getRLWithMaximumScore (firstN,RL_Set)

$$\text{RL} = \text{argmax}_{r\in RI\_Set} \sum_{f\in firstN} \sum_{r\in RI\_Set} \delta_r (f.Y) \times dur(f)$$

Return RL

The subroutines selectNFixations returns N fixations from the starting index. Similarly, getLargestXCoordinate returns the right-most fixation lying on an RL.

4 Validation

This technique was applied on Spanish and Danish translation and post-editing recording sessions from Translation Process Research (TPR) database. Qualitative analysis of the corrected data showed improvement.

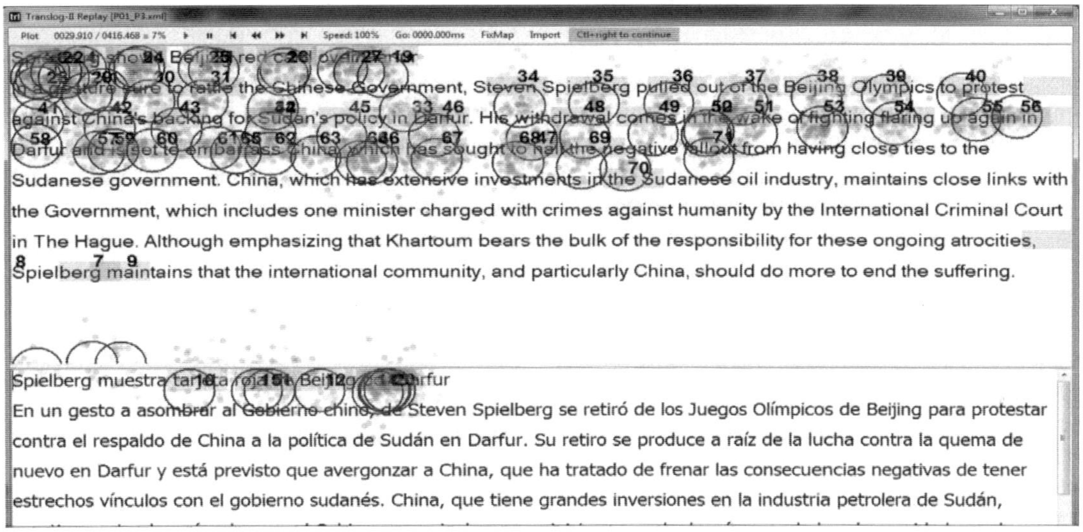

FIGURE 5 – Uncorrected fixations

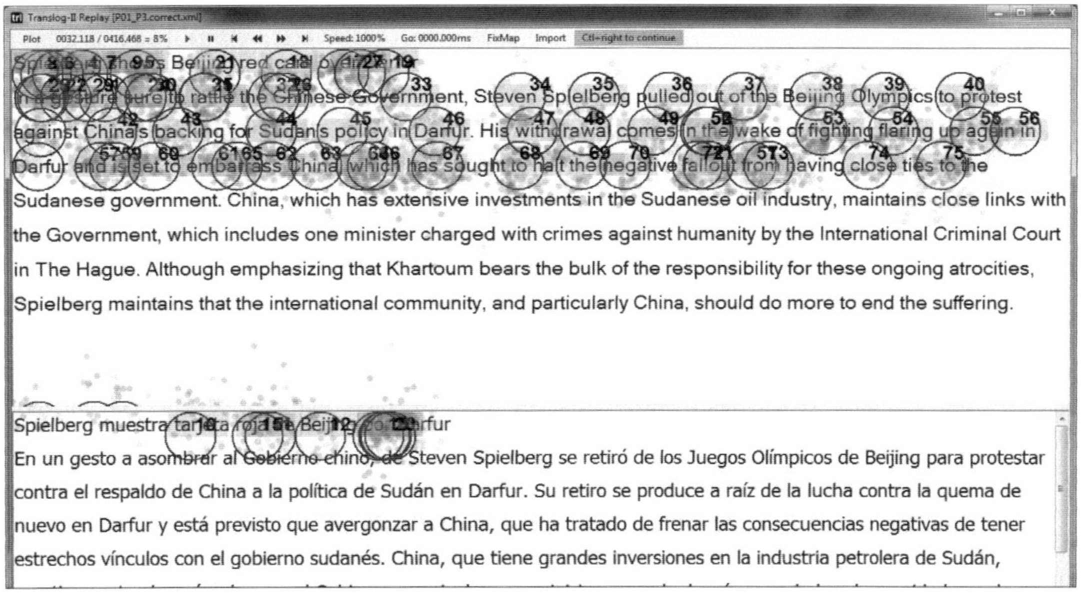

FIGURE 6 – Automatically corrected fixations

As we can see in the initial data (Figure 5), the fixation distribution is noisy and there is an overlap among fixations lying on line 3 and 4. After correction (Figure 6) the noise is significantly reduced. Fixations are labelled as per their temporal ordering.

5 Comparison with manual correction

We compared our output with manual corrections done for Spanish and Danish TPR data. Since our method shifts most of the fixations and manual correction only involves correcting only certain badly shifted fixations by mapping an appropriate word to the fixation, we checked for what fraction of manual correction could be successfully carried out by our method.

First, we mapped our fixations to the words on which they lie. Then from the original data we took the timestamp of those fixations which were corrected manually. For those timestamps we collected Fixation-to-word mapping for both the corrected versions and produced the Longest Overlapping Subsequence (LOS) between the mapped words. If the length of the LOS is more than the sum of the character counts of those two corresponding words, it is considered to be a valid correction.

For different values of N, we checked for the percentage of correction done with respect to manual correction. The results are shown by the following table

	N=3	N=6	N=10
Danish (10 sessions)	63%	83%	79%
Spanish (40 sessions)	55%	81%	81%

TABLE 1 – Automatic Vs Manual Correction

6 Conclusions

In this article, we presented a mechanism to correct systematic error associated with fixations by applying certain heuristics. The advantage of this method is, it can be applied both online (in the course of experiments) and offline. But the correction quality depends on the value of N and other parameters like initial experimental set-up and degree of randomness of fixations etc. It works best for shallow visualization studies; making it quite useful in studies like Translation Process Study, Sentiment Analysis etc.

There are certainly several factors for drift and imprecision apart from what we have taken into account. For instance, if the eye-tracker maps all gaze sampled, say 3cm below the intended location (because the head was permanently moved), all gaze samples are 3cm distorted, including the ones on the first N words in a line. Our algorithm fails to detect this. Of course, for the studies involving writing, we can get this constant drift (3cm) by comparing the cursor and the fixation positions during writing and finding out the average deviations. This is somewhat similar to RFL techniques assuming that a person's region of interest should not be very far away from the cursor position.

Our technique also fails if fixations are highly randomly distributed; which might be a case for studies involving detailed reading. In such cases, we also do not know the all the causes of the deviating fixations. Future work includes exploring and involving other case than just the two types of deviations that we took into account here. More cases and heuristics have to be included. A better validation technique has to be introduced as well.

References

Abrams, R. A., & Jonides, J. (1988). *Programming saccadic eye movements. Journal of Experimental Psychology: Human Perception and Performance*, 14, 428–443.

Hornof, A. J., & Halverson, T. (2002). *Cleaning up systematic error in eye-tracking data by using required fixation locations. Behavior Research Methods, Instruments, & Computers*, 34, 592–604.

Zhang, Y., & Hornof, A. J. (2011). *Mode-of-disparities error correction of eye-tracking data. Behavior Research Methods*, 43, 834–842. doi:10.3758/s13428-011-0073-0

Technologies, L. C. (2000). *The Eyegaze Development System: A tool for eyetracking applications. Fairfax*, VA

Carl, Michael (2012). Translog-II*: A Program for Recording User Activity Data for Empirical Reading and Writing Research*, In Proceedings of the *Eight International Conference on Language Resources and Evaluation, European Language Resources Association* (ELRA)

Carl, M. and Jakobsen A.L. (2009). *Towards statistical modelling of translators' activity data.* International Journal of Speech Technology, 12(4). http://www.springerlink.com/content/3745875x22883306/.

Carl Michael (2012). The CRITT TPR-DB 1.0: *A Database for Empirical Human Translation Process Research.* AMTA 2012 Workshop on *Post-Editing Technology and Practice* (WPTP-2012)

Špakov, O. (2007). GWM – *the Gaze-to-Word Mapping Tool*, available online at http://www.cs.uta.fi/~oleg/gwm.html.

Author Index

Aizawa, Akiko, 55
Alves, Fabio, 5

Bhattacharyya, Pushpak, 71
Blache, Philippe, 21

Carl, Michael, 71
Crocker, Matthew, 1

Gonçalves, José Luiz, 5

Hara, Tadayoshi, 55

Kano, Yoshinobu, 55
Kliegl, Reinhold, 37

Mishra, Abhijit, 71
Mochihashi, Daichi, 55

Rauzy, Stéphane, 21

Szpak, Karina, 5

Vasishth, Shravan, 37
von der Malsburg, Titus, 37